Get Organized

In today's world, we're often overwhelmed by our digital devices and the volume of available digital information. *Get Organized Digitally!* outlines a complete digital organizational system for the busy educator and helps you harness the power of technology to save time.

This book is your go-to source, presenting the "nuts and bolts" of exactly how to make technology work for you in both your personal and professional life.

Special features of *Get Organized Digitally!*:

- Details of how to get started with the best digital organizational tools available today.
- Principles of digital organization that make all the components of your system work together.
- Stories that inspire and show how technology can make our lives easier.

Time is the most precious resource we have; managing it well leads to greater productivity and less stress. *Get Organized Digitally!* shows educators how to harness the power of technology to spend time on what matters most—your school and your students.

Frank Buck is a veteran school leader with a career in education spanning almost 30 years. Today, he is a writer, speaker, and coach in the areas of organization, time management, and productivity. "Global Gurus Top 30" ranked Dr. Buck #1 in the "Time Management" category for 2019, 2020, and 2021.

Other Eye On Education Books Available from Routledge
(www.routledge.com/eyeoneducation)

Get Organized!: Time Management for School Leaders
Frank Buck

The Confident School Leader: 7 Keys to Influence and Implement Change
Kara Knight

**Creating, Grading, and Using Virtual Assessments: Strategies for Success
in the K-12 Classroom**
Kate Wolfe Maxlow, Karen L. Sanzo, and James Maxlow

**Leadership for Deeper Learning: Facilitating School Innovation
and Transformation**
Jayson Richardson, Justin Bathon, and Scott McLeod

**A Practical Guide to Leading Green Schools: Partnering with
Nature to Create Vibrant, Fourishing, Sustainable Schools**
Cynthia L. Uline and Lisa A. W. Kensler

**Rural America's Pathways to College and Career: Steps for
Student Success and School Improvement**
Rick Dalton

**Bringing Innovative Practices to Your School: Lessons from
International Schools**
Jayson W. Richardson

The Strategy Playbook for Educational Leaders: Principles and Processes
Isobel Stevenson and Jennie Weiner

Unpacking Your learning Targets: Aligning Student Learning to Standards
Sean McWherter

Strategic Talent Leadership for Educators: A Practical Toolkit
Amy A. Holcombe

Becoming a Transformative Leader: A Guide to Creating Equitable Schools
Carolyn M. Shields

**Working with Students that Have Anxiety: Creative Connections
and Practical Strategies**
Beverley H. Johns, Donalyn Heise, and Adrienne D. Hunter

Implicit Bias in Schools: A Practitioner's Guide
Gina Laura Gullo, Kelly Capatosto, and Cheryl Staats

Get Organized *Digitally*!

The Educator's Guide to Time Management

Frank Buck

Routledge
Taylor & Francis Group

NEW YORK AND LONDON

First published 2022
by Routledge
605 Third Avenue, New York, NY 10158

and by Routledge
2 Park Square, Milton Park, Abingdon, Oxon OX14 4RN

Routledge is an imprint of the Taylor & Francis Group, an informa business

© 2022 Frank Buck

Library of Congress Cataloging-in-Publication Data
Names: Buck, Frank, 1959– author.
Title: Get organized digitally!: the educator's guide to time management / Frank Buck.
Description: New York, NY: Routledge, 2022. |
Includes bibliographical references.
Identifiers: LCCN 2021030022 (print) | LCCN 2021030023 (ebook) |
ISBN 9781032015064 (hardback) | ISBN 9781032017075 (paperback) |
ISBN 9781003179719 (ebook)
Subjects: LCSH: Teachers–Time management. |
Time management–Computer programs.
Classification: LCC LB2838.8 .B84 2022 (print) |
LCC LB2838.8 (ebook) | DDC 371.102–dc23
LC record available at https://lccn.loc.gov/2021030022
LC ebook record available at https://lccn.loc.gov/2021030023

ISBN: 978-1-032-01506-4 (hbk)
ISBN: 978-1-032-01707-5 (pbk)
ISBN: 978-1-003-17971-9 (ebk)

DOI: 10.4324/9781003179719

Typeset in Optima
by Newgen Publishing UK

This book is dedicated to my wife and best friend, Davonia. Her love and encouragement over more than 30 years have been a constant source of joy and inspiration.

Contents

Meet the Author   xi

Introduction   1
The New Principal's First Day   1
Drowning in a Digital World   3
Baby Steps in a Digital World   4
A Worldwide Crisis   5
Why This Book?   5
Who Needs This Book?   6
What Should You Expect in This Book?   6

PART I: THE DIGITAL TASK LIST   9

1. **Your Digital Task List: All the Eggs in One Basket**   11
    Why Start Here?   11
    Sheldon's Story   13
    The Seven Essentials When Choosing a Digital Task Manager   15
    Remember The Milk   16
    Handling Settings   16
    Add Tasks   18
    Learn a Few Keyboard Shortcuts   20
    Next Steps   22

2. **The "Seven Essentials": What to Look for and How to
    Use Each One**   23
    Give Every Task a Due Date and Priority   23
    Add Repeating Tasks   25

Add Details in the Notes Section 29
Search 31
Sync Tasks Across All Devices 33
Send Tasks to Email 33
Enter Tasks with Your Voice 34
Next Steps 35

3. **Trap, Organize, Do: Do One Thing at a Time** 36
Trap: The Magic of the Inbox 36
Organize: The Magic of Planning 39
Do: Turning Plans into Action 44
Sheldon's Story Revisited 44
Total Control and Peace of Mind 46
Why Don't They Teach That in School? 46
Next Steps 47

PART II: DIGITAL NOTES AND DIGITAL DOCUMENTS 49

4. **Digital Notes: Information When You Need It** 51
Digital Documents v. Digital Notes: What's the Difference? 51
Jack's First National Conference 53
Getting Started with Evernote 56
Download the Mobile App 60
Evernote Home 61
What Other Notebooks Will You Need? 61
Next Steps 64

5. **Mastering Evernote: Features and Use Cases** 65
Journal 65
Viewing the Information in a Notebook 69
Organizing Notebooks with "Stacks" 70
Tags: Return to Grandma's Kitchen 73
Evernote Web Clipper 75
Forwarding Emails to Evernote 76
Saving Time with Templates 77
Tagging with Classroom Observations 78
Tagging with Lesson Plans 79
Search and Search Syntax 80

Links and Sharing   81
Clearing the .Inbox   84
Evernote "Free" v. Paid Plans   84
Why Don't They Teach That in School?   86
Next Steps   87

6. **Digital Documents: Retrieval Shouldn't Be a Safari**   88
    Uncluttering the Desktop   89
    Establishing Services Needed   89
    Documents   90
    Fingertip Files   94
    Current Projects   94
    Google Drive   96
    Link to It   101
    Why Don't They Teach That in School?   101
    Next Steps   102

PART III: ROUNDING OUT YOUR DIGITAL TREASURE CHEST   103

7. **The Digital Calendar: Building and Sharing Your Day**   105
    Calendars Then and Now   105
    New Demands on an Old Tool   107
    Calendar Sharing: The Baileys' Story   109
    Calendar Subscriptions   112
    Calendar Invitations   114
    Automated Schedulers: The End of Email Battleship   116
    The Superintendent Calls   119
    Why Don't They Teach That in School?   121
    Next Steps   122

8. **Email Mastery: The Hub of Your Communication**   123
    The Crazy Neighbor   123
    Savannah's Out-of-Control Email   124
    Favorite Gmail Tricks   131
    Do Unto Others   138
    Why Don't They Teach That in School?   139
    Next Steps   139

9.   **Digital Automation: Letting Tech Shoulder the Load**   140
The Stories We've Shared   140
If This Then That (IFTTT)   142
Voice Mail: It's Not 1984 Anymore   148
Feedly: For the Blogs You Love   149
Share with Remember The Milk   150
Text Expanders: Quicker and More Polite Replies   151
Gmail Templates   152
Gmail Filters   152
Voice Input: Why Type When You Can Talk?   154
Proofread with Your Ears   155
Write Like Hemingway   155
Hootsuite: Organizing Social Media   156
Why Don't They Teach That in School?   157
Next Steps   157

PART IV: CONCLUSION AND CHALLENGE   159

10.   **School Is Not a Place**   161
Where Did It Begin?   162
Where Are We Headed?   162
Sabrina's Journey   163
Your Journey   164

Appendix: Digital Services Referenced   166

Meet the Author

Frank Buck is a veteran school leader, having served as a central office administrator, principal, assistant principal, and band director during a career in education spanning almost 30 years. He has authored three previous books, numerous articles, and conducted hundreds of workshops and seminars within the United States and abroad.

Global Gurus has included Dr. Buck in their annual "Top 30" in the "Time Management" category each year since 2017. In 2019, 2020, and 2021, Global Gurus ranked him #1 in that category.

Dr. Buck resides in Pell City, Alabama. He writes, speaks, and coaches on organization, time management, and productivity. He may be contacted through his website: http://FrankBuck.org

Introduction

Having everything in its proper place allows us to enjoy what we have. That's why every New Year's Day we hear the common resolution: "This is the year I am going to *get organized!*"

The Information Age brings a challenge that will only become more significant going forward: "How do I get organized *digitally?*" Yes, we have the world's knowledge at our fingertips. We have unlimited storage capacity.

But what good is information if we can't find what we need when we need it? What good is it if the flood of information overwhelms us?

Would you like total control over your time and the peace of mind that nothing is falling through the cracks? It's going to take more than tips and tricks. It takes a system where the parts work together. That's what you find here.

Through the book, you'll meet some characters and learn along with them. That journey begins right now.

The New Principal's First Day

Sabrina's heart pounded as she walked across the parking lot. This day, her first day as principal, would shortly bring three surprises.

As she walked through the front door, the lobby seemed smaller than she remembered as a child. The bulletin board had been replaced by a digital display. The words and pictures that flashed across the screen stood

DOI: 10.4324/9781003179719-1

in stark contrast to the highly polished hardwood floor. That floor had greeted students for four generations.

The second surprise came as she approached the main office. There was the portrait hung proudly on the wall beside the office. The last time she saw that portrait was at the unveiling, the day of her grandfather's retirement.

Returning to the school where she had once been a student was special. Her grandfather having been its long-time principal made this opportunity the gift of a lifetime.

The Third Surprise

When she stepped into her office, the figure standing inside startled her. "Hi, Sabrina, remember me?"

After a few moments, it all clicked. "Dan! Is that you?"

Dan was straight out of high school the day her grandfather hired him as custodian for that school. Sabrina was in 2nd grade. He was now a few pounds heavier. The once-jet-black hair was now salt-and-pepper. Today, he is the district's maintenance supervisor.

"Remember this desk?" he asked. "You know, when your grandfather retired, this piece of history went into storage. With all the nicks from all the years, the missing handles, the drawers that no longer worked, and the finish worn straight through to the wood, it was time to retire his desk as well. It took six of us to lift it. They don't make 'em like that anymore.

"When we heard you were coming, the guys in the shop and I wanted to do something special."

Sabrina could almost see herself in the finish. The old oak desk looked brand new. His desk, her grandfather's desk, was now hers. The school he led is now the school she will lead in a world that has changed so much.

The Old Wooden Box

As Dan departed, Sabrina sat down at that beautiful desk for the first time since those visits to her grandfather's office. She noticed the wooden box on the corner of the desk. She remembered this ornate wooden tray from her days as a student. When she would visit her grandfather after school, his desk was always clear except for the family pictures on one corner and this box on the other.

It was always full of paper, but it seemed *everything he had to do was in that one box.* Today's mail, phone messages on little pink pieces of paper, notes from teachers, letters which needed replies—it was all there in one place. Getting to the bottom of it was always a challenge.

Between the paper in that old wooden box and the leather-bound planner he always carried, Grandfather seemed to stay on top of everything.

It all seemed so simple.

Drowning in a Digital World

Sabrina thought about her experiences as an assistant principal these last two years. Information came at her from all directions:

- Emails numbered over 100 every single day. Having to check four different email accounts made it all the harder.
- Voice mail kept the red light on the phone blinking constantly.
- Text messages spread across three different services made sure she would never have more than five minutes to concentrate on anything.
- Websites from her school system and state agencies were constantly updating information. She was responsible for knowing when something new appeared.
- Twitter was a great source for new information. But it all flew by so fast, and she could never find anything later.
- Blogs related to her profession provided helpful information. But how is a person supposed to check them all on a regular basis?

Sabrina had to look in so many places to find the incoming work that needed her attention.

On top of it all, she could never find digital information she already had:

- Every request for information started a 15-minute search through her out-of-control Google Drive. She knew she had saved it. She just could never find anything.

- When she went to a meeting, Sabrina would snap a photo of the whiteboard on the wall, a technique she learned from a tech-savvy friend. But the result just became one more scattered photo in her camera roll.

- She loved to read books on her tablet and enjoyed the ability to highlight passages. Sabrina always felt there must be a way to use those highlights. In reality, she never looked at them again.

- People would stop her in the hall and the conversation would result in information Sabrina needed to trap. But where? How would she find it later? How would she even remember she trapped that information in the first place?

- Putting her hands on any given email served as another frustrating time-suck.

Out of exasperation, she tried going back to paper. The result was even worse. Sticky notes lined her entire computer monitor, that is, except for the ones that had fallen on the floor. Her desk had become one big pile of paper.

"This time has got to be different," Sabrina thought. She thought about her grandfather, a man who looked at his circumstances and came up with procedures to handle those circumstances. *He did the best he could with what he had.* He had made it look so easy. She found it so hard.

Baby Steps in a Digital World

I've been in education since 1982 and remember the day the very first Apple IIe computer arrived at our school. Early on, I discovered a spreadsheet could serve as a gradebook. Before that day, one Saturday out of every six was devoted to the manual task of punching numbers into a calculator and copying names and averages in the various places needed in order for report cards to be distributed.

After that day, averages were always up to date. A quick sort and print were the only things needed to give homeroom teachers the grades from my subject. One simple spreadsheet application returned to me six full days a year. That's great time management. It was the beginning of a journey that has never ended.

Through the years, technology has been a friend. It's been a way to make difficult things easy and repetitive things to be done quickly.

In 2001, I set aside my trusty paper planner. The overnight transition resulted in a calendar, task list, and address book that were all digital. Suddenly my email inbox was empty every day. Along the way, I started sharing with others what I was learning. The desire then, and now, has been making life easier for school leaders everywhere.

A Worldwide Crisis

In March 2020, a global pandemic took us by surprise. It caused our school buildings to immediately shut their doors. Had it not been for technology, we wouldn't have had school.

For decades, we've debated the role of technology in education, "ed tech" as we often refer to it. All the while, for all too many, paper has remained the norm and we viewed technology as a nice "add-on." We rocked along with one foot in the boat and the other on the shore. When a virus changed our world, we changed how we worked.

We got digital devices in the hands of all students. Countless school systems parked busses in strategic places that allowed those busses to serve as hotspots. For years, we dreamed of making reliable Internet access available to all students. Overnight, it became a priority.

The average teacher became comfortable participating in and leading online conference sessions. School leaders began meeting with people all over the world without ever getting on an airplane. We all became "pioneers," feeling both the stress of the unknown and the excitement that we were pushing forward the frontiers of possibility.

We will never let ourselves go back to the days when technology was scarce. Our challenge is to learn to leverage the gift we have been given.

Why This Book?

We've never been better positioned in terms of hardware, software, and connectivity than right now. Technology has never been easier to use than right now. But we all need a guide to help us navigate the waters.

So much of our information arrives digitally. For that reason, *it just makes sense to fashion a system that allows digital information to stay digital*. This book gives you the framework to do exactly that.

You'll learn the tools you need, the strategies for using them, and how they can work together. The aim is to help you get organized, manage your time, and increase your productivity.

Organization is about putting things in the right place. Time management is about organizing our actions across time, so we get the right things done at the right time with the right tools. Technology is one of the best, but often underused, tools to make it happen.

Who Needs This Book?

This book is for those beginning a journey in educational leadership. It's also for those whose hair has grayed and feel this digital game has passed them by. It's for the mid-career educator who feels digital overwhelm with no help in sight.

This book is for the teacher who feels "school leadership" also means shaping the direction of education from the classroom. It's also for those who feel digital organization is a skill we must teach students and are looking for a framework to make it happen.

The countless educators with whom I have worked inspired this book. But if this book winds up in the hands of a doctor or a lawyer, a soldier or a priest, a homemaker, a grocer, a chemist, or a student with dreams as big as all outdoors, they are welcome to listen in and join us in the journey as we get organized digitally.

What Should You Expect in This Book?

You can expect three things. First, you get the "what," the overarching concepts and the best available tools as this book goes to press.

Second, you get the "how." You'll learn the "nuts & bolts" of how to get started with each piece of technology and how it will make a difference. Writing a book around the subject of technology is difficult. Technology changes. Good things are replaced by better things. Authors walk a fine line between being specific enough to be helpful and general enough to be eternal. In this book, we will err on the side of being specific. While tools change, solid principles remain eternal. As specific tools change, you'll understand the guiding principles behind what you're looking for in a replacement. You'll likely be delighted at the choices in this fast-developing arena.

Third, you get the "why." You'll meet characters and read their stories. Don't be surprised if their stories sound like your story. If I've done my job, you'll be inspired by the difference you see good tools making in the hands of dedicated people.

Part I of this book shows how to put everything you have to do in one place. In Chapter 1, learn exactly how to set up a digital task list. In Chapter 2, learn why each of the "Seven Essentials" for choosing a digital task list is important and how to use each one. In Chapter 3, learn how to plan your day in just a few minutes. Identify where progress will be made tomorrow and how to make sure good ideas for the future aren't forgotten. Learn how to plan projects and break them into small pieces that fit neatly into the day. Best of all, you'll see everything you have to do in one place. When we can see all our choices, we make better choices.

Part II is all about harnessing available information. Our information is only as good as our ability to find what we need when we need it. After implementing Chapters 4 and 5, you'll have an Evernote setup that makes entry easy and provides instant retrieval from anywhere. Chapter 6 presents a simple system for organizing digital documents. Too many people fail to understand the difference between the two concepts. You'll understand the difference and be able to use each one effectively.

Part III dives into a trio of important concepts. In Chapter 7, learn why a digital calendar is a must in our interdependent world. See how to set up sharing and automated calendar scheduling. Chapter 8 just might make email a friend again. You'll get your inbox empty each day. You'll also learn some Gmail tricks that take the drudgery out of email. Chapter 9 introduces services, most of them free, that save considerable time through the power of automation.

Part IV presents the final chapter of the book, Chapter 10. It makes the argument that "School is not a place." Technology allows us to be together even when we're apart. Get reacquainted with Sabrina, who you just met. See how she has used the concepts you'll learn to get organized digitally, to achieve total control over her time, and the peace of mind that nothing is falling through the cracks.

The Digital Task List

Your Digital Task List
All the Eggs in One Basket

What if you could start your day by instantly seeing a plan for that day already created? What if that plan included links to all the supporting information you would need? What if you could see that plan from any digital device you own?

What if you never had to rewrite a "to-do" list again? What if you could even add tasks for future days with voice alone? You can have it today.

 ## Why Start Here?

A good digital organizational system needs six basic elements:

1   **Calendar**. Tells us where we need to be.

2   **Task List**. Tells us what we need to do.

3   **Contacts**. Keeps up with information about the people in our lives.

4   **Notes**. Organizes fluid information (notes from phone calls, ideas, etc.)

5   **Digital Documents**. Stores files such as Word, Excel, Google Docs, etc.

6   **Email**. Serves as the hub of communication.

We start with the digital task list because it is woefully underused and has the power to put into one place everything that drives our days.

DOI: 10.4324/9781003179719-3

Ask Them

Ask a roomful of people the following question: "If you needed to look up a phone number, physical address, or email address, how many of you would consult something *digital* to do it?"

Watch every hand in the room go up. Everyone in that room would pull out a phone and have access to the information within seconds. When it comes to keeping "contacts" digitally, the average person has a good handle on that aspect of digital organization.

Gone are the days when people were keeping three address books: one on their phones for phone numbers, one in their email programs for email addresses, and a leather-bound one with physical addresses, phone numbers, and random information penciled in the margins. To go a step further, having access to those contacts from all devices is a concept most people have mastered.

Ask the same roomful of people this question: "If you needed to look up a calendar event or add something to your calendar, how many of you would consult something *digital*?"

Most hands would still go up, and the number grows with each year. But many people still look forward to buying a new paper planner as January approaches.

Finally, Ask This...

Ask that roomful of people one last question: "If you were going to add something to your to-do list, how many of you would consult something *digital*?" The number of hands raised dwindles.

Dig a little deeper with those who did raise their hands. Ask what software they use for their tasks. Get ready for two common replies:

1   I put my tasks on my calendar because I just don't have another place to put them.

2   I use the little yellow-legal-pad-looking thing on my iPhone. While that approach is fine for this afternoon's grocery list, it's not good for the tasks to be handled weeks or months in the future.

As you work through this chapter, you'll find a surprisingly easy way to keep up with everything you have to do. It will be much easier than sticky notes, random pieces of paper, or the illusion that somehow you'll just remember it all. To begin, let's introduce Sheldon.

Sheldon's Story

Sheldon's ability to motivate students and relate to parents made him a rising star in the classroom. Soon, he was being encouraged to pursue his administrative certification, which he did. When an elementary school principalship in a neighboring town came available, he applied. His personality impressed the hiring committee.

Sheldon had great plans for his new role as principal. But the first morning was occupied by one teacher after another dropping in, not only to meet the new principal but ask a favor or two. "I'll be glad to look into that and see what I can do," was Sheldon's general reply.

By lunchtime, Sheldon wasn't quite sure what promises he'd made. He grabbed a sheet of paper and began to pull a list out of his head. All the while, he felt sure he'd missed some things.

The Flood Continues

After lunch, Sheldon toured the building with the custodian. It seemed every teacher was taking this summer day to work in classrooms, meet the new principal, and add a few tasks to his ever-growing collection.

As luck would have it, every 15 feet, he picked up another couple of tasks. The paper where he had begun his list was back on his desk in the office. Sheldon reverted to his backup plan, one called, "I hope I can remember this."

An hour later, Sheldon was back in his office frantically racking his brain for the additional items to add to his list.

When the sun set, Sheldon was still at his desk. He managed to mark quite a few items off the list. Many more remained, and the page was beginning to be unreadable.

Sheldon hated the thought of hand-copying the remaining items onto a fresh sheet of paper. He began to get a sinking feeling that rewriting left-over tasks might turn into a time-consuming daily exercise.

Sticky Notes to the Rescue...Maybe

"Sticky notes!" he thought. "I'll write each task on a sticky note. When the task is done, I'll throw the note away. What's left is what I'll work on tomorrow."

He finished transcribing his tasks to the sticky notes just in time to answer a phone call from his wife. "When will you be home?" she asked. "Dinner is already cold."

Meeting His Colleagues

Shelton looked forward to this day. The superintendent had scheduled an administrative team meeting. Sheldon would meet the other principals and the central office team. His plan was to then return to his school and start tackling the sticky notes arranged in neat rows on his desk.

Sheldon would soon find out just how many tasks one inherits during an administrative meeting. In addition to three pages of notes on a legal pad, he had 15 new sticky notes shoved in his pocket and a three-inch stack of various reports and memos.

By the end of the day, most of the sticky notes which had been on the desk that morning were still there that evening. The collection had spread and now lined the computer monitor. A stack of papers started to grow on one corner of the desk.

On top of it all, he would be late for dinner again.

Fast Forward a Week

The days until the start of the school year began to dwindle. Everyone wanted a piece of Sheldon's time. Each day ended with more to do than when it began. Sticky notes had now covered the credenza and began to creep up one wall.

Each day brought meetings with teachers and parents. Sheldon felt like he needed to keep some sort of record but had no idea of how he would ever find any of it again.

Little things began to fall through the cracks. Teachers started leaving "reminder notes" just in case Sheldon lost the original stickies. Visions of big plans began to turn to hopes of just being able to hang on.

We Start Here Because the Improvement Opportunity Is Here

We have mastered the art of keeping a calendar. Showing up Tuesday at 9:00AM has never been the problem.

The problem arises with all the *things to do*. They live on sticky notes lining computer monitors. Much of the information is hand-copied from a computer screen. Even those who maintain a paper planner find themselves rewriting that list day after day.

So much of our information comes to us digitally. For this reason, fashioning a system which allows digital information to stay digital makes sense.

The Seven Essentials When Choosing a Digital Task Manager

The field is crowded, and each candidate professes to be simple enough to understand yet powerful enough to give you what you need. How do you choose? Figure 1.1 shows what to look for.

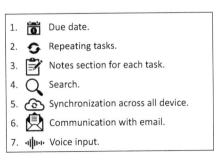

1. 📅 Due date.
2. 🔄 Repeating tasks.
3. 📝 Notes section for each task.
4. 🔍 Search.
5. ☁️ Synchronization across all device.
6. ✉️ Communication with email.
7. 🔊 Voice input.

Figure 1.1 Seven essentials when choosing a digital task manager

We will explore each of the "Seven Essentials" in Chapter 2. For now, it's time to "jump in" and start to get organized digitally. But first, let's make an agreement.

Remember The Milk

Rather than present many choices, let's go deep into one of the leading candidates. Remember The Milk (RememberTheMilk.com) is my personal choice. It's also the one I teach because even the free version offers all of the "Seven Essentials." Before reading another word, grab a computer and let's start to get organized digitally.

Handling Settings

Go to RememberTheMilk.com and create a free account. Upgrading later provides additional features. The free account is fine for the needs of most people.

As with any software, Remember The Milk has some one-time settings.

- Look for a downward-pointing arrow in the upper-right corner of the screen and click it.
- Click *Account Settings* and begin working through the menu items.
- In the "Accounts" menu, click on *Change photo* and upload a headshot. This photo shows up in various places as you work with Remember The Milk. This item also allows the username and email address associated with the program to be changed.
- The next menu item allows you to change your password at any time.

The "General Tab"

These settings will save time and eliminate repetitive entries every day:

- Start View: Today
- Default List: Inbox

- Default Due Date: Today
- Default Sort By: Priority
- Default Fields: Due, Repeats, Tags, URL, Give to
- Date Detection: On
- Private Addresses: On
- Release Channel: Stable

The screens for *Contact Preferences* and *Daily Digest* are self-explanatory. Personally, I don't see the need for either.

Sometimes, a task needs to be performed at a particular time. Remember The Milk allows you to set a *time* as needed. If the task has a time, an audible reminder a few minutes ahead of time is helpful. The control for that setting is here.

On the next screen, *Notifications*, check all the boxes.

Continuing with Setup: Email Tasks

The *Email Tasks* menu is gold. In your Contacts, create two new contacts, one for each of the email addresses you see.

I named mine "Remember Milk" for the first and last names of the contact and pasted the *Inbox Email* address into the contact. I then created a contact and named it *Milk Import*. The *Import Email* address gets pasted here.

Why the "Inbox Email" Is So Important

Any email sent to the special *Inbox Email* address shows up as a new task in Remember The Milk. That feature is extremely important in helping you stay on top of the "to-dos" that show up in your email.

When we talk about how to get email empty, the ability to forward an email into Remember The Milk is extremely important. The *Import Email* may or may not be useful. We will examine its role later.

Attachments

Pro account users are able to upload files associated with tasks. Remember The Milk handles this function by placing files in your Dropbox account or Google Drive. This menu option is where you grant Remember The Milk permission to place items in either of those accounts and link to those files.

The settings are done. Now the fun begins!

Add Tasks

Try your hand at adding a task. Pick something you need to do anyway: a phone call to make, an errand to run, a person to see. Click on the *Add a task* field and enter text. When finished, click the *Add Task* button or press *Enter* (*Return* on Mac). Figure 1.2 shows how the screen will appear.

Enter a second task. This time, watch what happens as soon as you enter the first letter. Figure 1.3 highlights the icons that appear. Mouse over each one to see what it adds to the task. You can choose a due date, priority, repeating pattern, assign the task to someone else, and more.

If you didn't choose any, simply type the task, and hit the *Enter* key, the task would appear in Remember The Milk in both the *Today* list with a due date of *today* and *no priority*. The task would also show up in the *Inbox*.

Put It All in One Place

Are you like Sheldon, one of those people who has reminders *everywhere*? Some are on sticky notes. Others are on random scraps of paper. Still others are stuck in a purse, wallet, or surround the computer monitor.

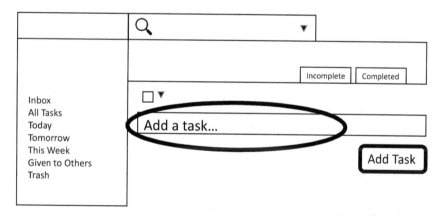

Figure 1.2 Adding a task

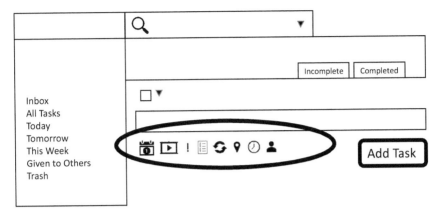

Figure 1.3 Adding attributes to a task

Still other reminders float around in your head. Still more are embedded in meeting notes in various legal pads.

Gather it all in a pile. Start putting those tasks into Remember The Milk. As new tasks come to mind, put them into Remember The Milk. From this day forward, promise yourself the days of random notes are over. Every task goes into the digital task manager.

Make Tasks Crystal Clear

Start tasks with a *verb*. Word the task so it is specific and doable in one sitting. *"Sally's birthday"* is a terrible name for a task. *"Call ABC Bakery to order cake for Sally's birthday"* is a great one.

As you enter tasks, use the icons to add due dates, priorities, repeats, etc. Remember, if you add no due date, *Today* becomes the default because of what you entered in the Account Settings.

Break Projects into Tasks

Look at your list and find any task that is actually a set of tasks rolled into one. Putting "Plan Sally's birthday" serves as reminder to work on that event. But what exactly will you need to do?

This birthday is an example of a *project* composed of a number of steps. Start thinking it through, and many tasks come to mind. Who will you invite? Will you need to print invitations? What decorations do you need to buy? Will you hire a magician, and if so, who? Later, we'll show you an approach for handling multiple projects.

Do the thinking on the front end. Throw the tasks in the list. The list does the remembering. As school leaders, much of what we do is not hard. *Keeping up with it all* is what's hard.

Learn a Few Keyboard Shortcuts

Click an icon below the task line and a list of suggestions appears. Figure 1.4 provides an example. Clicking on the *due date* icon inserts the caret (^) following by a list of possibilities. Another way to assign a due date would be to manually enter the caret followed by the date. Click *Enter* and Remember The Milk formats the date correctly. Click *Enter* again or click the *Add Task* button and Remember The Milk accepts the task.

Adding a priority works the same way. Manually enter an exclamation point and choose from the list which appears. Want to assign the task to someone else? While creating the task, manually enter a plus sign (+) and a list of the contacts added to Remember The Milk appears. Figure 1.5 shows a task including a date, a priority, and a person to whom the task is delegated. Clicking *Add Task* or *Enter* adds the task to the list.

Figure 1.4 First keyboard shortcut

Figure 1.5 Task with several attributes

Figure 1.6 Using Smart Add

Entering This:	Has This Effect:
^Tomorrow	Task will be due tomorrow.
^Feb. 23 or ^February 23 or ^2/23	Task will be on the upcoming February 23rd.
!1 or !2 or !3 or !4	Assigns a priority to the task.
*Every Tuesday or *Every Month	Assigns a repeating task.
Call Bob // Left a message	Creates a task "Call Bob" and creates a note that says, "Left a message. The note will be date/time stamped.

Figure 1.7 Keyboard shortcuts in task line

Using "Smart Add"

Do you like to use the keyboard instead of the mouse? Smart Add also allows for typing the date and time as part of the task. For example, try entering the task shown in Figure 1.6.

This ability to free-type a date or time in the subject will become extremely handy when we address adding tasks via voice.

Our Account Settings included a reminder five minutes before any task with a due time. Therefore, Remember The Milk will send the appropriate alert five minutes before the due time.

For other selections, adding a symbol followed by free-typing text will work, as in Figure 1.7.

The Desktop Application

Remember The Milk runs online. However, a desktop application exists, and it offers one distinct advantage.

To download the desktop application, open Remember The Milk. As you view the list of tasks, look at the links in the very bottom of the right-hand pane. One will say *Apps*. Click that link. On the page that opens, look for the download links for your type of computer. Download and install as with any program. The program will look like and operate just like the one from the Web.

Smart Add Hotkey: As Easy as a Memo Pad

To make using a digital task list something the average person will use, entering information has got to be as easy as jotting it on a memo pad. Voice entry into the phone is actually *easier* than a memo pad.

With the desktop application, one keyboard shortcut provides the same ease of entry from the keyboard. Open Remember The Milk with the desktop application. Enter the following keyboard combination:

- Windows: Ctrl + Alt + M
- Mac: Command + Alt + M
- Linux: Ctrl + Alt + M

A rectangular box appears in the middle of the screen. Key the task and press *Enter*. The box goes away, and the task is in Remember The Milk. Include any of the *Smart Add* features in the task line.

Next Steps

If you presently use paper to manage to-dos, examine what challenges you see in adopting a digital task list. Do you know someone who uses a digital task list successfully? Being able to "compare notes" with someone who has gone down this road is valuable.

We learn by doing. Before reading further, create your digital task list. The next two chapters will make more sense if you implement each concept as you read about it.

The "Seven Essentials"

What to Look for and How to Use Each One

There's no shortage of software on the market to manage "to-dos." But downloading a task management app doesn't make you organized any more than buying a paintbrush makes you a great artist. Great tools plus a great system for using them is the key to success. Chapter 1 listed seven essential items a digital task list should have. This chapter examines why each is important and how to use each of them.

Give Every Task a Due Date and Priority

Have you already set up an account in Remember The Milk and begun to add tasks? In the *Settings* menu, the recommendation was if no date was specifically assigned, the due date would default to *Today*. For our purposes, the due date answers the question, "When do I want to see this task again?"

Some tasks need to be completed as soon as possible. Others cannot or should not be done for days, weeks, months, or even years.

Do you have a passport? It's good for ten years. What's going to remind you nine years and several months from now that it's time to renew? Create the task now while you're thinking about it. Add a due date, even if that due date is almost a decade away. It's out of the way and off your mind. You earn the right to forget about it. On the appropriate date, the task is there.

DOI: 10.4324/9781003179719-4

Sort by Priority

Your *Today* view shows the items to accomplish on this day. But some of the items are critical while others could be done tomorrow with no harm. Some tasks can only be done at home. Others must be done at school. Segment the list by giving every task a *Priority*. Here is how I use mine:

1   **Priority 1**. My "Fab 5," the five tasks that either must be done at all costs or are highly profitable.
2   **Priority 2**. Tasks I want to accomplish in the *morning*.
3   **Priority 3**. Tasks I want to accomplish in the *afternoon*.
4   **No Priority**. Tasks I want to accomplish in the *evening*.

A classroom teacher could structure priorities this way:

1   **Priority 1**. My "Fab 5." Start on these upon arrival at school.
2   **Priority 2**. Tasks for the teacher's *planning time*.
3   **Priority 3**. Tasks for *after school but before leaving for home*.
4   **No Priority**. Tasks for the *evening at home*.

While looking at the *Today* list, sort it by priority. Click the gear icon and choose *Sort by priority*. The list will remain sorted this way.

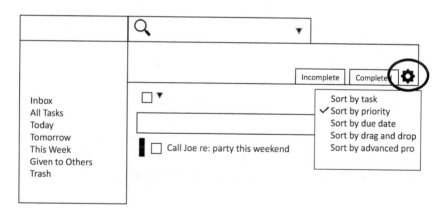

Figure 2.1 Sorting to make an organized list

What About Overdue Tasks?

Tasks not completed simply roll over to the next day. A *Priority 2* task left undone today will show up tomorrow in the *Priority 2* section and blend in with any other *Priority 2* task already scheduled.

You never have to rewrite tasks. You never have to copy and paste tasks. You never have to drag and drop tasks from one day to another.

Add Repeating Tasks

Education is probably the most cyclic business in the world. We start school every year, end school every year, and host the same events each year at the same time. Each example carries with it a set of "things to do."

What if you didn't have to rethink these tasks every year? What if these individual tasks came back to you each year at exactly the right time?

Likewise, we have tasks which repeat each month and each week. Identify those repeating tasks and add them to your digital task list. The task appears at the right time. Do it and mark it complete. The task disappears and resurfaces the next time it needs to be done. This one feature is a tremendous time saver.

What are the individual tasks we find ourselves performing for each of these repeating events during the year? The school business is full of tasks to perform the same time every year. For example, think about the many things that must be done every summer to get ready for the school year. Likewise, every school leader has tasks that repeat every month or every week.

Performing the tasks is not difficult. The tricky part is keeping up with the tasks and not letting things fall through the cracks.

What follows is a starter list of repeating tasks. These tasks are written from the standpoint of a principal. Many would be applicable to a teacher, counselor, central office administrator, or many other leadership positions.

Sample Repeating Tasks for Summer

- Revise faculty handbook.
- Revise student handbook.

- Analyze discipline statistics from previous year.
- Examine standardized test data.
- Draft plan for test-score improvement.
- Purge filing cabinet.
- Compose duty roster for coming year.
- Update custodial schedule.
- Compose master schedule.
- Assign students to classes.
- Prepare list of textbook fill-ins.
- Prepare annual budget.
- Order honor roll ribbons for coming year.
- Prepare list of needed office supplies.
- Order nameplates for all new teachers.
- Select mentors for new teachers.
- Organize evaluation forms for coming year.
- Schedule PTA officer meetings.
- Arrange for fire extinguishers to be checked and serviced.
- Schedule dates of assembly programs for coming year.
- Schedule dates for school pictures (fall, spring, Santa).
- Schedule severe weather drills, fire drills, and intruder drills.
- Schedule new teacher orientation.
- Schedule PTA meeting dates.
- Submit field trip requests for annual trips.
- Plan birthday gift idea for teachers.
- Plan staff development program for coming year.
- Compose press release regarding registration.
- Compose press release on new teachers.
- Compose communication to parents regarding registration.
- Compose monetary requests from PTA.
- Prepare "welcome back" letter to faculty.
- Prepare "welcome back students" post on website.

- Plan meeting with custodial staff regarding new assignments.
- Plan meeting with lunchroom manager.
- Plan meeting with counselors.
- Schedule parent volunteers to help with opening day.
- Test all bell schedules.

Sample Repeating Tasks for September

- Gather grading and discipline procedures from all teachers.
- Plan PTA Open House.
- Review progress reports to identify students already having difficulty.
- Draft talk for civic organizations regarding plans for the year.

Sample Repeating Tasks Just Before the Winter Break

- Compose winter break work schedule for custodial staff.
- Prepare Christmas or other holiday cards for faculty.
- Prepare Christmas or other holiday cards for key city leaders.
- Write thank-you notes for gifts received from staff and students.
- Be sure heat has been set correctly for long break.

Sample Repeating Tasks Each Spring

- Review with counselor plans for high-stakes test administration.
- Oversee intervention plan for students in danger of retention.
- Schedule end-of-year evaluations.
- Order certificates for Awards Day.
- Write Awards Day speech.
- Prepare presentation for local civic clubs on year's accomplishments.
- Secure recommendations for students needing to attend summer school.

- Select teachers for summer school.
- Compose annual discipline statistics report.
- Schedule end-of-year evaluation conferences.
- Prepare recommendations for teacher contract renewals and non-renewals.
- Prepare press release on scholarship recipients.
- Write press release on retiring teachers.

Sample Repeating Tasks Each Month

- Review school goals and plan tasks for their accomplishment.
- Examine financial statement.
- Compose newsletter.
- Write article for newspaper.
- Run progress monitoring report.
- Order supplies for school store.
- Examine playground equipment for needed repairs.
- Compose honor roll statistics.
- Print student birthday list for the coming month.
- Plan meeting with PTA president.
- Prepare remarks for PTA meeting.

Sample Repeating Tasks Each Week

- Examine reports from computer-assisted learning programs.
- Plan classroom observations.
- Examine attendance report.
- Compose weekly communication to faculty and staff.
- Compose weekly communication to parents.
- Send press release to newspaper re: school activities.
- List thank-you notes to write.

Use this starter list and then add your own items. Continue to add new repeating tasks as soon as they occur to you. Don't limit this feature to only work-related tasks. What home maintenance items need regular attention? What repeating tasks do you have surrounding your finances?

Start Delegating

When you get it all in the system, you begin to get an idea of the job's enormity. You'll begin to get an idea of what you must do, what things others can do, and what things don't need to be done at all.

Repeating tasks are prime sources of items to delegate. Because those tasks return again and again, taking the time to teach someone else how to do them becomes a huge timesaver.

Add Details in the Notes Section

Click on any task in Remember The Milk and the right-hand pane opens. This pane includes a "Notes" section.

Cedric's Story

Cedric is the Director of Human Resources. His tasks include many phone calls. He uses the notes section of tasks to put supporting information at his fingertips.

Organized school leaders plan their calls. They know what points they want to cover and what questions to ask. Cedric tried to keep all this information in his head. Later, he started making little agendas for phone calls on sticky notes. He often found it hard to find the right sticky note at the right time, especially if he was away from his desk.

Cedric began using the task's notes section. When he added "Call Bob" to his task list, he also entered in the notes section the items he wanted to cover when he connected with Bob. If he thought of more items later, he searched his list for "Bob" and added them to the notes section.

If he tried to reach someone and got voice mail, he would leave a detailed message. Cedric liked to keep a record of who he called and when.

So, in the notes section, he would put that he left a message. Remember The Milk adds a date and time stamp on each note. Cedric would sometimes leave several messages before making contact. If challenged, Cedric could quickly provide the date and time of each attempt.

Sometimes, Cedric needed to reference a particular email during a call. Searching Gmail for just the right email while the other party was on the phone was time-consuming and often embarrassing. Cedric learned that each Gmail message had its own link. From that day forward, Cedric would copy the link to the message and paste it in the notes section of the task. During the phone call, Cedric was one click away from having the correct email at hand.

Likewise, Cedric often needed to refer to a document during the phone call, a meeting, or during many planned tasks. Anything in his Google Drive, Dropbox, or OneDrive account had a unique link. Therefore, pasting the link in the notes section meant that when he started to perform the task, each piece of reference information was only a click away.

When Cedric finds an article online, he often lacks the time at that moment to digest it and wants to return to it later. He used to add such articles to his "Favorites." But he ran into a problem. Cedric would forget to look at the Favorites. Plus, over time, he would forget to "unfavorite" articles after reading them. As a result, "Favorites" quickly got out of control.

Now, when Cedric comes upon an article to read later, he creates a new task. He pastes the title of the article as the task name. He then pastes the link to the task in the notes section and saves the task. Cedric now moves on and can be confident that he will see the article on his list and read it when he has more time.

The Place for Anything Related to the Task

Your digital task list is the central place for everything you have to do. The notes section of that task is the spot for every piece of supporting information related to that task. You saw examples from Cedric's day. What can you add?

Do you have a picture that needs to be reframed? It's been sitting behind a door at home for four months. Add a task to your list: *Take Picture to ABC Frames*. Saturday is a good day for that to happen, so add Saturday's due

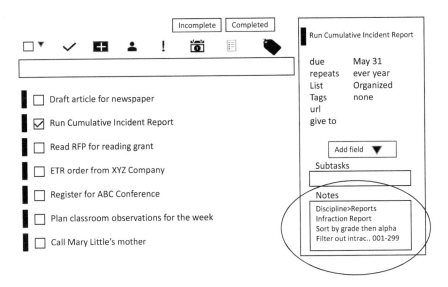

Figure 2.2 Using task note

date. In the notes section, remind yourself: *Picture is behind door going to garage.* Forget about it. On Saturday, your list reminds you of what to do and points you to the supporting material you will need.

Could that supporting material include a file folder? If so, put that information in the notes section along with its location.

Do you have a task, perhaps a report, that only comes around once a year? Remembering the details of how to prepare that report can be elusive. The next time you do that report, take a few seconds to put those details in the notes section of the task. You already know how to make a repeating task. Next year at this time you see the reminder to do that report. You also see the step-by-step instructions for how to do so. Figure 2.2 shows what might go in the task note when the task is to run a certain discipline report.

Search

Enter a word or phrase in the search window at the top of the screen, as shown in Figure 2.3. Press *Enter.* Remember The Milk returns any task including the search terms. We will use the search box to find any task even if it's not on our list of tasks to do today.

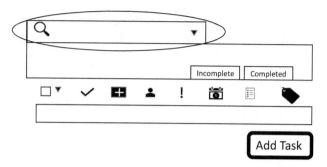

Figure 2.3 Searching the task list

Using Key Words in Tasks

Using due dates and priorities puts tasks in order. They make it easy to plan the day in a nice flow. What about when the unexpected happens?

Cedric arrives at a school for a meeting with the principal. When he arrives, Cedric learns the principal is dealing with an issue and will need another 45 minutes. What will Cedric do with this time? He has his phone, so he can make phone calls if he knows which ones he needs to make.

Cedric opens Remember The Milk on his phone and enters *Call* in the search. He has been consistent about putting the word "call" somewhere in any task that involved a phone call. So, his search returns all the calls he needs to make regardless of due date.

Likewise, when someone calls Cedric or shows up unexpectedly, Cedric can search for that person's name and find all the tasks related to that person.

Cedric routinely loans books to others, places orders with vendors, and leaves voice-mail messages for others. He needs a way of keeping up with what he is expecting to receive from other people. He uses the abbreviation *ETR* (standing for "Expect to Receive") as a part of any task where someone else is responsible for the next step. When he searches Remember The Milk for *ETR*, Cedric has a comprehensive list of what he is waiting on from others.

Need a More In-depth Search?

Click the drop-down to reveal the *Search Wizard*. Click the *Search notes* box and Remember The Milk searches for the text not only in the names of the task but also in the task notes. Click *Add another criteria*. Click the *Choose* drop-down to gain an idea of the choices available.

Sync Tasks Across All Devices

Download Remember The Milk on your mobile devices. Log in with the same username and password as when you created your Remember The Milk account. Because it is Web-based, the program is available on any computer connected to the Internet. Data entered anywhere syncs everywhere with no action required.

On the mobile app, swipe to the right to mark a task complete. Swipe to the left to postpone to a future date. Press and hold on a task for other options to appear.

Send Tasks to Email

How many emails sit in your inbox day after day because they are reminders of things you have to do?

Usually, they're poor reminders. You read five paragraphs to figure out that the "to-do" is "Call Mary." Wouldn't it be nice if the email's subject line was something that was actually helpful? How about something like "Call Mary"?

When handling those types of email, take one of two actions:

1 Do the task right now and be done with it.

2 Put the task on your task list.

Vow never, ever to just let "to-dos" sit in the inbox. We wind up reading and re-reading. We wind up thinking and then rethinking what needs to happen first, second, third, etc. The task sinks farther down the page and on to the next screen, and the next. No wonder we're drowning in email.

Special Email Address

Click the gear in the upper-right corner and return to the account settings. Select *Email Tasks*.

```
To: yourname+54321@rmilk.com
Subject: Call Bob ^11/15 !2

Dear Frank,

I would like your input on the ABC Project. I am out of town right now.
Is there any way you could call me on November 15?
I will be in the office all day. Best number is (987) 555-1212.

Thanks,
Bob
```

Figure 2.4 Email just before forwarding to task list

Two addresses appear. Highlight and copy the one marked *Inbox Email*. Go to your contacts and create a new contact. I called mine "Remember Milk." His first name is "Remember" His last name is "Milk." In the email address for this contact, paste the inbox email you copied a moment ago. Save the contact.

Any email sent to that address will appear in Remember The Milk. The subject line of the email becomes the name of the task. The body of the email appears in the notes section of the task.

When an email needs future action, forward it to that special email address. Before sending, change the subject line to reflect the action you will need to take.

Also, you can add other elements to the subject so that the task shows up on the correct day and the correct part of the day.

In Figure 2.4, the email is ready to send. The "to" is your special address. The subject line is clear. This task is a phone call to Bob to happen on November 15. The *!2* indicates *Priority 2*. For me, *Priority 2* indicates tasks for the morning.

On November 15, "Call Bob" is sitting on the list for that morning. Clicking on the task provides the needed details.

Enter Tasks with Your Voice

Input has always been the difficult part of using a mobile device. Typing on a small keyboard or small screen pales in comparison to the full-sized keyboards on our computers.

On the keyboard for your mobile phone, look for a key that resembles a microphone. Tap the icon in Remember The Milk to create a new task. Instead of keying the task, use the microphone key to speak it. The text will appear wherever the cursor is located.

In Chapter 1, we talked about *Smart Add*. As you speak the task, also speak the due date:

- Call Samantha Tuesday
- Call Samantha tomorrow
- Call Samantha March 22

Both Android and iOS users who have the Remember The Milk Pro account can download a widget for the home screen. Without even opening the app, tap the microphone icon on that widget and speak the task.

iOS users can enter tasks via Siri. After downloading the Remember The Milk app, watch for a prompt to allow Siri to access Remember The Milk.

Next Steps

One of the problems email poses is that so many of them include things we have to do. Pick two or three such emails and forward them to your digital task list using the instructions you read in this chapter.

Block out some time to brainstorm all the repeating tasks which come to mind. Enter them in your system. While you won't think of them all, you give yourself a big head start.

Download the mobile app. Practice voice input. New things take practice, and with practice comes ease. Our aim is to make voice entry so easy it becomes reflex.

Trap, Organize, Do
Do One Thing at a Time

Much of the overwhelm we feel is because of trying to do everything at the same time. This chapter outlines three distinct components of workflow. In the third component, "Do," you'll also master the fine art of project management.

Have you ever tried to rub your stomach and pat your head at the same time? Doing either one is easy. Trying to do them both at the same time is the challenge.

Watch people try to juggle a notebook, calendar, to-do list, and address book all at the same time. Details fall through the cracks and the stress level in the room rises.

Do one thing at a time. Trap all the information in one place. Later, put things where they belong. Finally, do the things you put in your system.

Remember at the beginning of the book that wooden inbox Sabrina's grandfather had on the corner of his desk? He used it to trap all incoming paper. In our digital world, we need exactly the same thing. In this chapter, we look at how to trap incoming information. Then, we organize it and decide exactly what we will do and when. Finally, we do the work.

Figure 3.1 provides a partial list of the places where "to-dos" for the school leader appear. Most of those listed are digital.

Trap: The Magic of the Inbox

In Remember The Milk, every new task goes into the inbox:

DOI: 10.4324/9781003179719-5

• U.S. Mail	• Online News Articles
• Phone Calls	• Pocket Memo Pad
• Voicemail (Landline)	• Drop-In Visitors
• Email attachments	• Twitter
• Professional Blogs	• Text Messages
• Voicemail (Cell)	• Slack (Other Messaging App)
• Announcements on Work Website	• Memo Pad by the Phone
• Email (How Many Accounts?)	

Figure 3.1 Partial list of places work appears

1   Tasks keyed into Remember The Milk.

2   Tasks forwarded via email.

3   Tasks entered via voice.

4   Tasks others assigned to you.

5   Tasks added through automation (which we will cover later).

Peace of mind comes from the confidence you can throw anything at Remember The Milk and it's never lost. Hear a good idea to put in place at school? Throw it in Remember The Milk. Come across a good article on a website you would like to read later? Throw the title and URL into Remember The Milk and rest assured it's there for you when you want to read it later.

We don't have to "do" everything the moment it arrives. All we have to do is have a single place to trap tasks. When we have that place to trap it, we earn the right to forget about it and continue with the important task in which we were engaged.

Let's look at the various places we could find a newly added task:

1   **At the top of the screen**. The new task appears for approximately ten seconds. Clicking on it will open the task for editing. This feature is helpful for adding details in the task notes.

2   *All Tasks*. This button in the left-hand pane shows every task in Remember The Milk. To see all tasks that have been completed, look for the *Incomplete* and *Completed* tabs at the top of the list. At present, completed tasks are saved for seven days for users of the free account and forever for users of the Pro account.

3   *This Week*. If the due date is within the next seven days, the task appears here.

4   **Today**. Any task with today's due date appears here. Any overdue task also shows up here. If the due date was for tomorrow, the task would appear in the *Tomorrow* list.

5   **Inbox**. The inbox is a place to see anything new, regardless of the due date, entered since the last time the user cleared the inbox.

Back to the Inbox

When the day comes to a close, look at the inbox. Are the tasks worded clearly? If not, take a moment to reword a task so it will be easy to understand and easy to do when it's time to execute on it. Look at the due dates. Make any changes. Look at the priority for each task. Make changes as needed to shift tasks from one part of the day to another.

When everything in the inbox looks good, empty it all in mass. To do this, we're going to create one more "list."

Remember The Milk provides two "lists" by default: *Personal* and *Work*. I don't use them. I like to see my entire day in one list. Tasks for the evening will appear at the bottom of the list in *No Priority*, so they are not going to be mixed in with tasks for the workday anyway. I recommend deleting one of the lists and renaming the other *Organized*. You will see drop-down arrows allowing these changes.

Clear the Inbox Daily

1   Look at the inbox every day.

2   Examine the wording for clarity. Change any due dates and/or priorities as needed. If the task will repeat, be sure the repeating pattern is correct.

3   When everything in the inbox looks good, move all of them together. To move them, place a check in the box at the very top. All tasks in the inbox will now show a checkbox. Mouse over the menu which appears and select *Move to*. From the drop-down, select *Organized* as your list. Hint: A keyboard shortcut is available. After putting a checkbox beside each item, hit the *M* key (for *Move*) followed by the *O* key (for the first letter of the desired

list). So, pressing *M O Enter* moves all tasks from the inbox to the *Organized* list.

Organize: The Magic of Planning

Plan Tomorrow Today

With a digital list, you never rewrite a task. However, you will do some rearranging. In the evening, take a few minutes to structure the next day for success.

Examine what's left over from *Today*. Each task will automatically remain on the list for the following day. However, some items may need to be assigned to other days. Place a check mark beside any item that needs a different due date or priority. Change the due date, postpone the due date, or change the priority for all of them at once.

Remember The Milk's keyboard shortcuts make these changes easy:

- **D for *Date*.** Select a new date and all checked items receive that due date.

- **P for *Postpone*.** This function also changes due dates but does so proportionally.

- **1, 2, 3, or 4 for *Priority*.** Place a checkmark beside several items and press "1." All selected tasks now become *Priority 1*. Likewise, the numbers 2, 3, and 4 would change the priority on selected items to *Priority 2*, *Priority 3*, or *No Priority*.

Next, examine what's already planned for *Tomorrow*. What tasks are already waiting for you? Do any need to be moved into the future? Which ones need to have their priorities changed? Put checkboxes in front of those tasks and handle changes in mass.

"Batch" Similar Items

"Batching" is a time-management technique that refers to performing similar tasks back to back. It takes little more effort to make a batch of three dozen cookies as it does to make a single cookie. Yet the results are extremely different.

Scheduling a number of errands back to back reduces the total time. Making a series of calls takes less time than if each one was intermingled with other types of task. As you plan your day, look for ways to batch similar items.

Saturday tends to be a good day for me to run errands. When I add an errand to Remember The Milk, I generally assign a date of Saturday and run all errands in one batch. To go a step further, assigning them all to *Priority 2* means they all show up on Saturday's list for the *morning*.

Many "expect to receive" items have no hard due date. Anything where I would be expecting a response within the week gets a due date for the upcoming Friday and given a priority of *Priority 3*. On Friday afternoon, I check on the status for all of them.

Break Projects into Small Pieces

Projects are different from other tasks on the list. Checking off a single task does not complete a project. Various authors have addressed ways to break down projects into small components that fit into our schedules.

Charles Hobbs, in his hallmark book *Time Power* (Hobbs, 1987), wrote of a pyramid which begins with "Unifying Principles" and works its way through several levels until we get to entries in the "Daily Action List." In *To Do—Doing—Done: A Creative Approach to Managing Projects and Effectively Finishing What Matters Most* (Snead & Wycoff, 1997), the authors talk about gathering project information in the back of a paper planner but identifying the small actions, entering them on specific daily pages, and linking those actions back to the project. *Making Ideas Happen* (Belsky, 2012), talks about "breaking projects into primary elements" (pp. 34–37) and each action is assigned to a particular person (p. 41).

We complete projects through *multiple steps*. Let's look at two approaches for handling projects. One assumes you are able to use "subtasks," a feature present in the Pro version of Remember The Milk and many other task managers. The second approach assumes you do not have the capability to use subtasks.

Project Planning Using Subtasks

Regardless of which method is used, start by defining the *goal*. What will be true when the project is completed? Examples might include the following:

- Math curriculum guide has been published.
- Treehouse has been built.
- Car has been purchased.
- Graduate school acceptance has been achieved.

Let's pick an example outside of education, perhaps the "treehouse" project. The kids have been asking for a treehouse and the parents don't know the first thing about treehouses.

Start by entering the goal as a task in Remember The Milk: *Treehouse has been built*. We talked about beginning tasks with *verbs*. My advice is to begin goals with *nouns*. Phrase the goal as a statement which is either *true* or *false*. When the statement is *true*, the project is complete. As long as the statement is false, there is still more to be done.

What are the steps involved in building this treehouse? These will be the subtasks. At the outset, you probably don't know them all. If a couple of friends have built treehouses for their children, phone calls to them would be easy first steps. List them as subtasks. What about an online search for information? Make it a subtask. A trip to the library would likely surface a good book or two on the subject. Do as much thinking as possible on the front end. However, don't worry about having to know all the steps at the outset.

Assign dates to the overall task (building the treehouse) and each subtask. Making the phone calls could have a due date of today. The trip to the library might be good for Saturday.

What date will we assign to the goal of building the treehouse? Pick a date when you would like to review the entire project again. I like to review current projects each weekend, so for me, the due date would be the upcoming Saturday or Sunday.

Project Planning Without Subtasks

Subtasks make it easy to plan many steps in advance, give each step a date, and let the software handle the rest. You will see what you need when you need it.

But even without subtasks, we can use a technique that lets you see the goal and see where you are on each project at the same time. I devoted an entire chapter to this topic in *Get Organized!: Time Management for School Leaders*, 2nd edition (Buck, 2016).

- Start by defining the *goal*. What will be true when the project is completed? That goal becomes the task.

- Place an *xx* to the left of the goal.

- To the left of the *xx*, put the next step toward reaching the goal. That next step will start with a verb and be something easily doable, such as a telephone call.

- Do you know any other next steps at this point? Maybe, and maybe not. If you do, list those in the notes section of that task.

- Do you have any more information about the goal? During your phone call or research, you will likely generate notes. Put those in the notes section of the task.

- Give the task a due date. This date will be the date you want to perform that next step, such as the phone call.

- When you complete that next step, highlight and delete just the next step. You are left with the *xx* and the goal.

- Your job is now to figure out what comes next and put that step to the left of the *xx*.

- Assign a new due date for when you plan to accomplish that next step.

- The entire project is handled with one task. At all times, you see the goal and the next step toward completing it side by side and separated by the *xx*. All the information about the project is in the notes section of the task.

One nice thing about this technique is the ease with which a person can make a quick list of all projects. Search for *xx*. Since every project has those letters in the task list, that search shows a list of all projects. The user sees every goal along with the next step toward completion.

Those who have read David Allen's *Getting Things Done* (Allen, 2015) will recognize the emphasis on defining what the final result will look like and the next step toward getting there.

The Master List: Planning the Week and the Month

You saw how to handle tasks such as errands and "expect to receive" tasks that have no specific date assigned. We all have many tasks or projects that just need our attention "sometime." How do we handle those?

The upcoming Sunday holds my "Master List" of tasks or projects for the next week. If I have extra time during the current week, I can click the *This Week* button and scrolling to Sunday provides a list of tasks to grab and reassign to the current day. Outside of that, when Sunday rolls around, I am looking at a list of tasks and projects. I make decisions about specific days and parts of the day for each task and make those changes in mass. Some tasks are simply forwarded another week by changing all their due dates to the next Sunday. I am building the following week and doing it with intention.

Likewise, the last day of the current month holds my Master List for the next month. I can always click the *All Tasks* button and select some tasks or projects to accomplish early. When the last day of the month arrives, I make decisions about specific days to schedule each task for the upcoming month. Many tasks will be pushed forward a month by postponing the due dates in mass. I am building the next month with intention.

All your choices about how to spend your time are in front of you. And when you can see *all* your choices, you make *better* choices.

Assign Tasks to Others

Wise school leaders delegate. If others around you also use Remember The Milk, you can assign tasks to them and vice versa.

Imagine a principal and assistant principal, a principal and an administrative assistant, or a husband and wife. Each person would have the ability to add tasks to the other person's list. Think of how many little pieces of paper and how much mechanical conversation could be eliminated.

In the *Contacts* area, click the "+" and enter an email address. If the person is not already a Remember The Milk user, he/she receives an invitation to create an account.

To assign a task to someone, put a check mark beside the task. Select *Give to* either from the icon at the top or the field in the right panel. The other person receives a notification to click and "accept" the task.

On a similar note, think about people to whom you would give permission to add to your list, but they don't use Remember The Milk. That was the situation for Sheldon.

Do: Turning Plans into Action

An organized task list sets up the day for success. Concentrate on the "Fab 5," your top five priorities for the day. Not everything on the entire list will get done, but that's OK. Continue tomorrow and stack one successful day after the other.

In summary, a good workflow, whether it's paper or digital, has three parts:

1   Trap: Write it down, or key it in, or paste it all in one place.
2   Organize: Put it in a logical order.
3   Do: Do the work.

Sheldon's Story Revisited

Since starting with Remember The Milk, the sticky notes had disappeared. Sheldon picked up one after the other and "spoke" each task and a due date into Remember The Milk.

Sheldon started keeping Remember The Milk open on a browser tab throughout the day. He was never more than one click away from his list. Because his phone was always with him, his plan for the day was always with him as well thanks to the Remember The Milk app.

Forwarding emails to Remember The Milk has been a gamechanger. Sheldon mastered the art of reading an email once, deciding on the action, and forwarding it to Remember The Milk. Being able to add a date and priority on the front made planning execution easier.

Looking at Remember The Milk provided order to his day. He could see his "Fab 5," the tasks he wanted to handle during the morning, afternoon, and evening. Having all the details in the task notes meant he never had to search for information when it was time to act.

Sheldon loved to spend time in classrooms. Since his phone was always with him, the ability to speak tasks into Remember The Milk was easy. He would make a note of repairs, log requests from teachers, and trap all the ideas that came to him as he watched students in action. For him, all this really did become as easy as jotting it on a memo pad.

One thing bothered Sheldon. Every day his administrative assistant handed him phone messages on little pink pieces of paper. If only he could figure out a way to make that process interface with his digital task list. Then, an idea came to him.

What if he could expand on the idea of forwarding emails? Sheldon jotted down his Remember The Milk email address and gave it to his administrative assistant. "When you take a phone message for me," he said, "instead of a paper message, you can just send an email to that address. It will automatically show up as a task for me in Remember The Milk. Whatever you put in the subject line will become the name of a task for me. All of the details in the body of the email will show up as a note for that task. In your email contacts list, just add this new contact. Name it something like 'Sheldon Milk' and enter my Remember The Milk email address in the appropriate field. Having that email address in your contacts lists will allow it to auto-populate." His assistant duly added the address to her contacts.

Sheldon left the next day for a conference. He had been looking forward to this national conference for months. But he always dreaded walking into his office the first day back. His desk was always covered with little message slips.

Later in the day, Sheldon touched base with his administrative assistant. "It's been a busy day," Sheldon's assistant said. "Yes, we had a couple of situations, and you'll have some phone calls to make when you return. But it's nothing that can't wait. And don't worry. I've sent the details to your Remember The Milk email address."

When the call ended, Sheldon opened Remember The Milk on his phone. He tapped the *This Week* button and began to scroll. There were the calls, each on specific days and with priorities assigned. Sheldon begins to click on each one. In the notes section of each task are the related details.

When Sheldon returned to work, his desk was clean. His mind was clear. His list was organized. He was ready for a productive day.

Total Control and Peace of Mind

What does your digital task list give you?

- Everything you have to do is in one place.
- Tasks appear when they need to appear.
- Repeating tasks are on autopilot.
- You can find anything instantly.
- You have a strategy and tool to get tasks out of email.
- You can even enter tasks with your voice as they occur to you.
- Worrying about what is falling through the cracks is banished.

When will you "finish" everything on the list? Hopefully never. If we stay relevant, each day brings new opportunities and exciting ways to make a difference. Let's not view the task list as something that must be finished. Instead, view it as something to be enjoyed.

Why Don't They Teach That in School?

The amount of information coming at today's students dwarfs anything from previous generations. We can help them design a system where everything is in one place.

Students will simply try to remember it all unless someone shows them a different way. Many schools use a paper assignment book, the one place for students to trap everything. But like any other skill, it must be taught. It begins with teachers telling students what to write and where to write it. We banish the sentence, "Now don't forget" and replace it with, "Open your assignment books, and here's what to write down for Thursday."

Students love their phones. Why not help them turn their phones into productivity tools? For most students, putting their to-dos as well as their appointments on the calendar would be sufficient. For those who need more, Google Tasks is practically built into Google Calendar. Older students would love the power a full-featured task manager such as Remember The Milk provides.

The most basic principle of organizing our commitments can be summed up in the words: *Write it down*. To go a step further, it all needs to go in the same place. Whether it's a pocket memo pad, an assignment book, or a mobile phone, the fine art of trapping everything in one place is a skill that pays dividends for a lifetime.

Next Steps

We began this book with three chapters devoted to digital tasks for a reason. This tool forms the foundation of everything to follow. The digital task list is the one place for everything you have to do. It drives your actions for today and allows you to plan your tomorrows. Take time to reread, thoroughly digest, and practice the concepts from these chapters.

We used Remember The Milk as an example. We've gone into enough detail you should be able to begin using it effectively. Other digital lists will also work. Use the "Seven Essentials" to guide your selection.

Notice the reaction of others as they see you entering tasks with your voice. Notice their reaction when they can tell you are not only listening but are translating *what you have heard* into *what you are going to do*.

Recognize your role as a model. Who are the next logical people to learn what you are learning here? What is your role in helping students develop the skills of trap, organize, and do? These are skills that will bring success throughout life.

References

Allen, D. (2015). *Getting things done: The art of stress-free productivity.* Viking.

Belsky, S. (2012). *Making ideas happen: Overcoming the obstacles between vision and reality.* Portfolio/Penguin.

Buck, F. (2016). *Get organized!: Time management for school leaders* (2nd ed.). Routledge.

Hobbs, C. R. (1987). *Time power.* Harper & Row.

Snead, G., & Wycoff, J. (1997). *To do—doing—done!: A creative approach to managing projects and effectively finishing what matters most.* Fireside.

PART

II

Digital Notes and Digital Documents

Digital Notes
Information When You Need It

Technology has put the world's knowledge at our fingertips. We even call the time in which we live the "Information Age." We rely on our digital tools to save relevant knowledge for later.

But the information we save is only as good as our ability to find it when we need it. In this chapter, you'll learn the difference between digital documents and digital notes and why you need both. You'll also make a start on building your own system of digital notes, one you will use every single day.

We're as likely to need a piece of information during a bus ride as we are to need it while at our desks. Our information must be accessible from anywhere. Likewise, we must be able to add new information or make changes to existing information from anywhere.

Our days move quickly. So, we must be able to share information with others instantly and from anywhere. Gone are the days when we say, "I'll get that to you when I get back to the office." Why not handle the task in the moment and be done with it?

 ## Digital Documents v. Digital Notes: What's the Difference?

We begin by learning the difference between the two concepts. You'll also see the case for why we need both.

DOI: 10.4324/9781003179719-7

Differences Used to Be Easy to Understand

The school leader before the 1980s understood the difference between the two concepts:

Characteristics of documents:

- Produced on a typewriter.
- Composed on paper of a standard size (such as 8½ x 11 inches).
- Considered more "formal' in nature.
- Pages stapled or bound together.
- Thought of as being in its "final form."
- Stored in file folders inside filing cabinets.

Characteristics of notes:

- Handwritten.
- Written on paper or index cards of any size.
- Considered more "informal" in nature.
- Pages could be loose, paper clipped, inserted into a loose-leaf note-book, or entered directly into a bound journal.
- Thought of as being "fluid" with annotations in margins.
- Often found at hand in a desk drawer or in a briefcase

Grandma understood the difference. She jotted her recipe for that special dessert on an index card. That card went into a 3 x 5 file box with the index cards for other recipes. Grandma was producing "notes."

What happened when the local chamber of commerce decided to publish a town cookbook? Grandma hauled out the typewriter. She carefully typed a few of her best recipes on pages measuring 8½ x 11 inches and having one-inch margins all around. She submitted her "documents" for inclusion in the cookbook. Grandma understood the difference between "notes" and "documents."

The 1980s, 1990s, and Muddied Water

Personal computers allowed the user to compose and edit on screen. Mistakes became easy to correct. Liquid Paper was no longer a necessary office item. The air of permanence about the document diminished. Loading the digital document, editing, and reprinting was easy.

The advent of the internal hard drive diminished the need for printing at all. Users created digital filing systems. Suddenly we were creating folders within folders within other folders and storing digital documents in hierarchies. The hard drive became the "digital filing cabinet." The computer was the center of a person's digital life.

Little by little, all digital information became "digital documents."

Confession Time: I Didn't Understand It Either

The first time I heard the word "Evernote," the person explaining it said it was "a way to organize your information."

"I don't need it," was my response. "My information is meticulously organized in file folders within file folders on my computer."

"But you can get to it from anywhere," was the comeback.

"I have a Dropbox account," I retorted. "Anything I need to access from anywhere can go in there."

I didn't get it. I didn't understand the difference between "digital notes" and "digital documents." Neither did I see the need for a difference. That opinion has since changed.

Jack's First National Conference

Jack is a third-year principal. He has been looking forward to his first national conference for months. As soon as the exhibits opened, Jack goes straight to the aisle for the playground vendors. New playground equipment is a major project for his school. Jack's plan is to gather some detailed information.

One piece of equipment catches Jack's eye. Like most people in today's world, his inclination is to take out his mobile phone and snap a picture. While most people's camera rolls feature an assortment of random pictures, Jack is different.

Photos

Jack touches an icon on the home screen, creating a new note in Evernote. He taps the camera icon, points it at the equipment, and taps the button to take a picture. He takes several pictures from different angles. All pictures are saved in the same note.

The vendor hands Jack a flyer. Jack realizes just how much paper a person could collect at a conference, so he declines. Instead, he taps the camera icon again and snaps a picture of the flyer. Still in the same note, Jack takes a photo of the vendor's business card.

Audio

The vendor senses Jack's interest and begins to talk about the features of the equipment. The information is good, but it is too much and too quick for Jack to comprehend.

"This is great stuff," Jack said, "but I'm afraid I missed some important points. Would you mind going over the information again?"

Jack hits the microphone button within that Evernote note. As the vendor speaks, Jack is making an audio recording with that same note.

Text

Some other thoughts are rolling around in Jack's head. While still in that note, Jack hits his keyboard's microphone button and speaks those thoughts aloud. Evernote transcribes his words into text.

As Jack walks away, he has a wealth of information from the last few minutes. It's all trapped within a single note.

Synced in His Account

That evening, Jack boots his laptop and opens Evernote. In a notebook he called .Inbox are all the notes created during the day. He created a note for each of the day's breakout sessions. He sees the notes for conversations he had with two authors.

Most importantly, the note from the playground vendor is safe and sound in his Evernote account. It is viewable from any computer with Internet access. It is also viewable from his mobile devices.

Jack notices several words the voice recognition had not heard correctly. So, he corrects the typos. While thinking about this vendor, he navigates to the company's website. He downloads a PDF with additional information. Jack clicks and drags the PDF into the original note. He also downloads a PowerPoint presentation from the company's website and saves it to the laptop's desktop. He clicks and drags the PowerPoint file into the body of the same note.

This single note, one representing his encounter with this vendor, now includes photos of the equipment, a business card, two flyers, a PowerPoint presentation, audio, and his own text. His information is in *one place*, not *all over the place*. Jack understood the power of having a tool designed for digital notes.

Shared with His Superintendent and Assistant Principal

Jack knew his superintendent would be interested in this information. He selects *Share* and *Email a copy*. The superintendent opens the email and views the photos, flyers, and PowerPoint presentation. He listens to the audio. He can read Jack's dictated notes. The superintendent is able to experience all this information without even having an Evernote account.

Jack's assistant principal, Michael, is an Evernote user. Jack selects *Share* and even gives Michael the rights to edit the note. Michael saves the note in his account. As the two men collaborate on this playground project, they can both add to the note.

Now I Get the Difference

Could Jack have done the same thing without a mature notetaking application such as Evernote?

Sure, mobile phones have always had cameras, voice recorders, and some type of notetaking app. At the playground booth, the photos would have gone to the camera roll. The audio would have been saved to the voice recorder. The notes that occurred to Jack would have been saved to the notes app. The information would have been spread across three different places.

It's no wonder people are good at getting things into their software and terrible at finding the information when they need it.

Getting Started with Evernote

In this chapter and the next, we focus on Evernote as the tool for handling digital notes. Comparable tools include Microsoft OneNote, Google Keep, and Apple Notes.

The easiest way to understand Evernote is to use it. With this book in hand, open a browser and navigate to evernote.com. The page lists the types of account and the features of each. Choose the "Free" plan. A user can upgrade at any time. Be sure to record your username and password. Later, the mobile app will need these same login credentials. Evernote will ask several questions about usage. The software is then ready to use. Because it is being accessed from the Internet, the information is available from any computer that has Internet access. Use your login credentials, and you can access your information from anywhere.

Your First Notes

Think of a "note" as an index card. To create the first note, click the *New Note* button. Evernote also provides the ability to start with a "template." With the free plan, you can choose from a library. With one of the paid plans, you can create and save your own templates. Perhaps you have a form you use frequently for meetings or lesson plans. These would make excellent templates.

Evernote has the common features found in any word processing soft-ware. Use the menu at the top of the note to change the font, size, style, or layout. Insert tables, attachments, or photos with the blue *Plus* button.

For the first note, let's start with a challenge for all of us: keeping up with the random numbers and codes in our lives. Title that first note "Personal Information A–C." Begin listing in alphabetical order those little bits of information that begin with A through C. Some of mine include the following:

- Air filter dimensions.

- Alfa discount code for automobile rental.

- American Airlines Advantage number.

- Battery size for car key fob.

- Copying machine code.

Click the *New Note* button and create another note: "Personal Information D–F," and then others for G–L, M–P, Q–T, and U–Z. Here are some of the bits of information you may have:

- Delta Skymiles number.

- Driver's license number (and for your spouse and children).

- Hilton Honors number.

- License plate number for automobile (and other automobiles in the household).

- NAESP membership number (and membership numbers for all other associations).

- Paint color code for office walls (or for any other part of the building or home).

- Passport number (and passport numbers for spouse and children).

- Printer toner number.

- Tax exempt number for school.

- Zoom personal meeting room link.

This list is just for starters. Pull together the various numbers and codes in your life and put them here. The next time you check into a hotel and the front-desk associate asks if you have your membership number handy, say, "Of course I do," and open Evernote. The next time a website asks for a membership number, copy and paste from Evernote. Say goodbye to keying it in from a collection of cards stuck in the back of a drawer.

Your First Notebook

Notes live in notebooks. In fact, the notes you just created live in a notebook Evernote created. In the left-hand pane, click *Notebooks*. In the upper-right portion of the screen, click the *New Notebook* button. Name the new notebook *Personal_Information*. Notice the underscore. To make searches easier later, I recommend *notebook names do not include spaces*.

Next, move the notes to the *Personal Information* Notebook. Evernote gives you two ways to do that:

1 **Use the icon at the top of the note.** At the top of the note is the name of the notebook where the note is currently located. Hover the mouse just to the right of it and select *Move note* when that option appears. Select the *Personal Information* notebook and click the *Move* button. Do the same for the other notes.

2 **Drag the note to a different notebook.** In the left-hand pane, look for *Notebooks* and click the arrow point beside it. A list of all the notebooks will appear. Click and drag each note into the *Personal Information* notebook.

What else might you add to the *Personal Information* notebook?

- **Bio**—How many times does someone need to introduce you and on the spur of the moment asks what they can say about you? Create that short narrative now. The next time this situation occurs, open the note on your phone and hand it to the person introducing you. Every time I apply to speak at a conference, the application asks for a bio. When it happens, I go back to that same note to copy and paste into the form. I have a bio with one variation that is 30 words long, another 90 words long, and another 140 words long. I have one variation if the presentation is for music educators, others for school administrators, and others for the business world. Once I create one, I never have to recreate it ever again. It goes into this same note.

- **Contact QR Code**—If someone wants to add me to their Contacts, I pull up this note and let him/her scan the QR code and save.

- **Family Tree**—Determining who is related to whom and how can get tricky. Once you get it figured out, writing it down keeps you from having to rethink it later.

- **Important Legal Documents**—Would you like to have a scan of your passport's photo page on you at all times? The same question goes for your driver's license, automobile insurance card, voter registration card, medical insurance card, birth certificate, and marriage license. The same holds true for those documents for other family members. Sure, you have the numbers in your personal information notebook, but sometimes having a picture of the document is valuable. Scan each of these items to your computer's desktop. Evernote allows you to click and drag them right into the body of the note.

Before, we move on, have I mentioned someone, or have you thought of something to scan and add to Evernote yet you do not have it to hand? In other words, you will need to *remember* to come back and add it?

Maybe you'll remember; maybe you won't. That's why the digital task list is so valuable. Create a task and list the items to gather. Let your digital task list do the remembering.

Your Second Notebook: .Inbox

An inbox of any sort is the place to trap new information. In this book's Introduction, we read about the decorative wooden inbox Sabrina's grandfather used. In Chapter 1, we learned that new tasks entered into Remember The Milk go into an inbox. We're all familiar with the email inbox.

Now it's time to create an inbox for Evernote and make it the "default notebook." All new notes will go there first.

Click *Notebooks* in the left-hand pane. A list of notebooks appears, as shown in Figure 4.1. Let's rename the one Evernote created for you. As this book goes to press, it's called *First Notebook*. Click the three dots on the right-hand side of the screen and choose *Rename notebook*. You would see a choice to *Set as default notebook*. It's already the default notebook, so that option does not appear. Each time you create a note, it automatically saves this default notebook unless you specifically make another choice.

.Inbox is the name we will choose. Notice the dot in front of the word. The dot will cause that notebook to sort to the top of the list.

During that day, every note you create will go to the *.Inbox* notebook. At the end of the day, examine that notebook. Decide on any action you need to take related to those notes. Enter those actions into your digital task list. Often a note is added in haste and requires some "cleaning up." One of

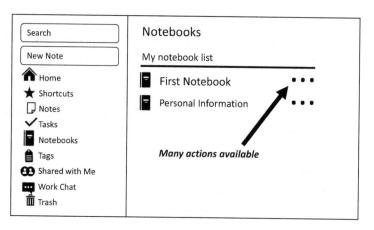

Figure 4.1 Viewing notebooks in Evernote

the beauties of this software is the ability to edit and improve a note on the fly. Changes automatically save. The last step is to move each of the notes from *.Inbox* to the appropriate notebooks.

Download the Mobile App

So much of the Evernote advantage comes from having information from anywhere. Before creating more notebooks, download the Evernote mobile app to the phone. It is available for both Android and iOS.

The app will ask for your Evernote username and password. The information begins to sync. The notes and notebooks created in Evernote Web show up on the mobile app. Changes made on one device sync to the Evernote account in the cloud and are available on any other device where Evernote is installed.

Evernote offers several plans. As this book goes to press, a free Evernote account allows use of Evernote Web from any computer with Internet access. In addition, the user can download software to one device. A mobile phone is the most logical choice. A paid account allows the user to download the mobile app to other devices, such as a tablet. A paid account also allows the user to download Evernote for Windows or Evernote for Mac. This software installs directly on the computer and provides additional features.

Evernote Home

By this time, you have hopefully done some "hands-on" work in Evernote. When you open Evernote the next time, you will likely see *Evernote Home*. It resembles a dashboard of widgets.

First, view the most recent notes with which you have worked. Clicking on a note from Evernote Home will open it. Very often, the note you need now is the one with which you just worked. Another tab reveals "Suggested Notes," notes with which you interact often.

Second is the *Recently Captured* widget. The newest information added via the Web Clipper, adding through a voice note, etc., shows up here.

Third is the one I feel to be the most beneficial. The *Scratch Pad* is like the memo pad which lives beside the telephone. When you need to jot a name or number, the Scratch Pad provides a digital place to do so. Often, we trap thoughts on a paper scratchpad and then key that information into something digital. The Evernote Scratch Pad allows the information to begin in digital form. You can then copy and paste that information anywhere else. This handy tool holds up to 300 characters. The three dots in the corner of the widget allow the information to be converted to an Evernote note for permanent storage.

What Other Notebooks Will You Need?

As with any filing system, it's helpful to have a model when getting started. What follows are suggestions. Also, look at your present filing system for paper, the folders created on your computer's internal drive, and the files created in any cloud storage such as OneDrive, iCloud, or Google Drive. Some of those file names are likely candidates for notebook names in Evernote.

Since you have just created a notebook and renamed another, now is a good time to keep rolling and add more notebooks. In a moment, we'll take a deeper dive into two of them.

Notebook Suggestions for Work

- **Athletics**—This is a place for game schedules for your school, nearby schools, honors, or any other information you would like to have at hand regarding this area of life.

- **Current_Events**—When you see a good article on a trending topic, use the Web Clipper to save it to Evernote. (Again, notice the underscore. Notebook names contain no spaces.)

- **Emergency**—What do you do when a bus accident occurs? What phone numbers do you need to have handy for various emergencies? This information will be with you everywhere. Find that information in seconds.

- **Fundraising**—Each note would be a project under consideration or one that had been completed in the past. Include such things as the name of the vendor, sales rep, profit margin, links to brochures, and prize information.

- **Grants**—One note could be a long list of potential grant opportunities with a link to the website. Create a note for each grant under consideration. Include contact names, phone numbers, and email addresses. If known, include contact information for other schools that were awarded this grant in the past.

- **Journal**—A description of this notebook will follow.

- **Observations**—Likewise, you will shortly see a detailed description of this notebook.

- **PTA**—A list of officers and their contact information. Plans for PTA projects. Links to important documents related to PTA, such as the PTA constitution.

- **Professional Development**—Create a note for each speaker or consultant under consideration. In each, include contact information, the topic, cost, and notes from communication. Include a note for each professional development opportunity being planned locally.

- **Public Relations**—Create a note for the local paper with names of key people and their contact information. Create a similar note for each television or radio station. If the school has a long-term plan for improving this area, this notebook is a place to put the plan and strides made.

- **Safety**—One note could link to the school's safety plan. Any URL pasted into a note becomes a clickable link.

- **School_Law**—One note could be a "cheat sheet" on the landmark Supreme Court cases related to education. Many conferences include good school law sessions. Each session becomes a new note. This notebook is a place for them.

Notebook Suggestions for Home

Evernote isn't just for school. Use it to hold important personal items.

- **Address_Lists**—Mine holds a PDF of the church directory, contact information for officers of different organizations, and a PDF of the homeowner's association directory. When one becomes outdated, trash it and replace it with the updated copy.

- **Automobile**—When we buy a new car, a note goes here with such information as the VIN number, where we bought the car, the date, the salesman, the price, and the initial mileage. When we sell the car, we return to that note and put the trade-in information. When we put a new set of tires on the car, a new note holds the relevant information. Each trip for repair or routine maintenance becomes a new note.

- **Book_Notes**—I enjoy reading on my tablet's Kindle app. The ability to highlight notes and view all highlighted text at one website is great. Put what if I no longer have access to that information? Using the Web Clipper (which we discuss later), I send those highlighted notes to Evernote. Each note contains the highlights from a different book.

- **Home**—A home is a huge responsibility. We have subscription services for television, lawn maintenance, and pest control, just to name a few. How quickly can you put your hands on phone conversations, important emails, and invoices? You come across information on taking care of your lawn, tips on buying clothes, stain removal, or how to choose a security system. I use tags (which we discuss later) to further organize the collection.

- **Your Child's Name**—Label a notebook with the name of each child. A trip to the doctor becomes a new note. When the child wins an award, create a new note with the details. Include a photo. The organizational meeting for little league baseball becomes a new note where you'll list the names and contact information for the coaches and paste a copy of the practice/games schedule. Create a note for the child's height and weight and keep a log over time. (When we talk about "Stacks" in

Chapter 5, if you have more than one child, you'll likely want to combine the notebooks for your children into one "Stack.")

- **Your Pet's Name**—Each pet gets a notebook. As this book goes to press, over the last 30+ years, nine Shetland Sheepdogs have called the Buck household their home. In each dog's notebook is a note with information about acquiring the dog. Another note is a picture of the bag of food the dog eats. Another note lists the dog's weight over time. Each trip to the vet becomes a new note. (If you have or have had multiple pets, you will likely also create a "Stack.")

Next Steps

Reread the chapter and work through the setup. Before reading further, create the notebooks that seem applicable and create notes.

In Chapter 5, we explore more advanced elements and provide additional examples of how Evernote fits into your day.

Mastering Evernote
Features and Use Cases

Chapter 4 presented a strong foundation for getting started with digital notes. With a logical system of notebooks, knowing where to put each note becomes easy. This chapter explores the final two elements of the Evernote structure: stacks and tags. We'll see examples of how Evernote can be used in schools by the principal, a teacher, or a student.

Two notebooks were mentioned in Chapter 4. Let's begin by exploring them in more depth.

Journal

Have you ever used a paper journal to record the events of your life? Over time, that journal chronicles the people you meet, the accomplishments you achieve, and miscellaneous happenings around you. In Evernote, the *Journal* notebook will do the same. Because Evernote is available on mobile devices and voice input is so easy, you will likely find no need to carry a paper journal anymore.

The People You Meet, the Friendships You Form

The busy school leader comes in contact with many people and has significant conversations every day. What if there was a way to organize all that information? The *Journal* notebook is the perfect place.

DOI: 10.4324/9781003179719-8

Create a note for a person and save it in the *Journal* notebook. Title it with the name of that person. Include contact information and notes of interest about the person's family and career. Add links to the person's website and LinkedIn profile. Copy and paste a headshot into the note.

What did you talk about during that initial conversation? Create a date stamp (Shift + Alt+ D on Windows or Shift + Command + D on Mac) and enter the highlights from the conversation. Jot down each significant interaction in that same note. The most relevant information will likely be the newest interactions. Therefore, the best approach is to enter new information "bottom up." Add the newest interaction at the top. You see a history of your significant interactions in reverse chronological order. Each entry carries a date stamp.

When an old college friend calls, search for that friend's note in the *Journal* notebook. You used to have a hard time remembering the names of his children because you only talk to him about twice a year. Now, the names of the children, along with the years of their births are in your friend's note. You see notes from your last conversations and can weave those details into this call.

When you send someone a thank-you note or receive a gift, update that person's note in the *Journal* notebook. Add the date stamp and notate the entry. If you wish, include a picture of the thank-you note or item you received. Open the note on your phone, tap to place the cursor where you would like the note to appear, and snap the photo.

Did one of your friends win an honor? Include it in the person's note. Include a link to the newspaper article about it or copy/paste the text into the note.

When a person I know passes away, I make it a point to find that person's obituary and paste it into their note. The obituary tends to be an excellent summary of his or her life.

Over time you develop a rich, fully searchable history of the conversations you've had and the events that have shaped the people you know.

Observations

Visiting classrooms is one of the essential jobs of a school leader. How can you keep up with who you have visited and what you saw? Create a notebook and label it *Observations*.

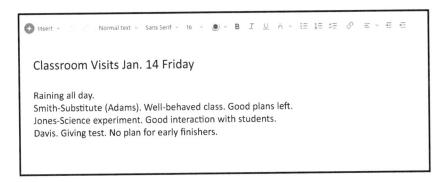

Figure 5.1 Notating class visits in Evernote

Jack is a principal who makes it a point to visit each classroom each day. He creates a note and titles it *Classroom Visits* and includes the date as part of the note title, as shown in Figure 5.1. As he walks from one classroom to the next, Jack pulls out his phone and adds a sentence or two about anything notable. He touches the microphone key on the keyboard and whispers information into his phone. Evernote turns his voice into text.

Several times a year, Jack conducts a formal observation with each teacher and stays for 30–60 minutes. For these visits, Jack creates a separate note. For this purpose, he uses his laptop and starts by choosing a "template," a topic we'll discuss later in this chapter.

Today is an observation in the choral room where the 7th grade girls' chorus is preparing for their fall concert. Jack creates a new note. He titles the note with the name of the teacher, the subject, and the date and time. He starts to key his thoughts into the note he created.

The teacher sings a line for the students. Jack touches the microphone within Evernote to start an audio recording and capture the teacher's beautiful voice.

However, Jack is also bothered by a vocal tick. The teacher begins almost every sentence with "You know." Jack thinks, "I am sure she has no idea she has developed this habit. If she could only hear what I am hearing, she would surely correct this practice."

He taps another icon from within Evernote, and the device's voice recorder begins recording the teacher's instructions. Because the recording is happening within Evernote, the results are saved as part of the same note.

When Jack is ready to move to another class, everything about that observation is in this one note. Every comment he keyed, audio recording he captured, or photo he took is saved together. The note saves to the .*Inbox* in Evernote. Jack can view and edit the note from his office computer.

Situations to Handle: Vandals Strike Again

On the way back to the office, one of the custodians informs Jack he has found evidence of a break-in. Vandals busted a window and gained access to a storage area at the rear of the school. They spray-painted hate speech on one wall and turned over two bookcases.

Jack calls the police to file a report. As he waits for their arrival, he creates a new note in Evernote on his phone. He titles it "Storage Room Vandalism" and taps an icon, bringing up the camera on his phone. He takes several pictures of the vandalism.

When the police arrive, he keys the names of the officers into the note. Together, they think through next steps that will help them solve the case. Jack taps the microphone icon on his phone's keyboard and dictates his thoughts into the note. Evernote turns his speech into text.

When the police leave, Jack calls his superintendent. She does not answer, so he leaves her a voice-mail message and says that he will email details. Jack taps the note he took regarding the vandalism. From the menu, he selects the option to "share" the note via email. He chooses his superintendent as the recipient.

Meetings, Meetings

Next on the agenda is a meeting of principals at the central office. Jack's paper journal had always served him well, but now he uses Evernote instead. As the meeting begins, Jack creates a new note, titles it "Principals Meeting" and takes notes as needed. Like most of these meetings, he inherits "to-dos." He adds those to his notes, marking each task with a checkbox.

Random Papers

Jack manages to escape his meeting totally free of papers. On his way out the door, one of the supervisors hands him the agenda for the next Board of

Education meeting. Not wanting to keep up with this loose piece of paper, he opens Evernote on his mobile phone, and scans the document the same way he would take any photo.

Viewing the Information in a Notebook

One feature that separates digital notes from digital documents is the ability to access the entire body of information at once. With digital notes, seeing information does not involve opening and closing documents.

Want to view the contents of a notebook? Click on its title in the left sidebar. In the middle, scroll through the notes in that notebook and see a preview of that note without even opening it. If the note has an image, Evernote includes a thumbnail in the preview. That visual element is extremely helpful in finding what you need. Click on a note and view the full note.

At the top of the note list is the ability to sort the notes by title, date updated, or date created and to filter the notebook. Personally, I like to let Evernote sort by the date updated. So often, the note you need to work with is the note you most recently accessed. Evernote tends to work like your brain. By the same token, clicking on *Notes* shows a list of notes starting with the one most recently updated and works all the way down to not touched for a great while.

Shortcuts

Each user has some frequently accessed notes. The same could be said for notebooks. In the left-hand pane is a menu item called *Shortcuts*. It's a place for the most commonly used notes, notebooks, tags, stacks, and saved searches. How can you add something to Shortcuts?

Open a note and click the three dots in the upper-right corner. *Add to Shortcuts* is one of the selections. Click on *Notebooks* in the left-hand pane. Beside any notebook, click the three dots to see *Add to Shortcuts*.

When we talk about organizing digital documents, you'll read about *Fingertip Files*. In Evernote, *Shortcuts* serve the exact same purpose.

Organizing Notebooks with "Stacks"

Think back to your college days. You had a notebook for the history class, another for the general science class, and another for the foreign language class. What would you have if you placed all these notebooks one on top of the other?

The answer is "a stack." In Evernote, that's exactly what you have. A "stack" is a group of notebooks.

Your Children and Pets

Jack has three children: Allison, Jessica, and Zeke. He created a notebook for each child. Notebooks appear in alphabetical order. The *Allison* notebook is located near the *Automobile* notebook. The *Jessica* notebook is just above *Journal*. The notebook for *Zeke* is at the bottom of the list. Wouldn't it make more sense to have all three notebooks together? A "stack" serves that purpose.

The same argument holds true for pets. The notebooks for Champ, Fluffy, and Rover are spread throughout the alphabet. A "stack" will put them together.

Creating a Stack

In the left-hand pane, click *Notebooks*. A list of all notebooks appears. Each has a set of three dots beside it (Figure 5.2).

To create a stack for the three children, perform these steps:

1   Click the three dots to the right of the *Allison* notebook.
2   Choose *Add to stack*.
3   In the submenu that appears, choose *New stack*.
4   Provide a name for the stack, such as *Children* and save.
5   We now see the new stack. Clicking the arrow to the left of the name displays the notebooks inside the stack. We have one: *Allison*.

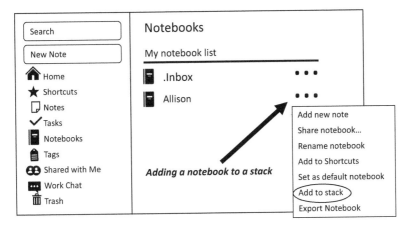

Figure 5.2 Adding a Notebook to a stack

6   To add *Jessica* to the *Children* stack, click the three dots beside that notebook. Select *Add to stack*. Choose the desired stack. Do the same with the *Zeke* notebook.

7   A second way to add a notebook to a stack is to drag and drop. Having created a *Children* stack, click on the name *Jessica*. Drag it on top of the *Children* stack. The notebook is now a part of that stack.

Notice the left-hand sidebar. *Children* would appear in the list of notebooks. Clicking the arrow point to the left reveals the notebooks in that stack.

Once a stack is created, dragging a notebook into or out of a stack can also be done within the left sidebar.

Curriculum

Jack is strong in the area of curriculum. He often clips articles from the Web and stores them in Evernote. He is an avid reader of books related to curriculum and uses Evernote to take notes from them. He learns new ideas about curriculum at workshops and stores those ideas in Evernote.

Jack created a notebook in Evernote for each subject area. He also created curriculum-related notebooks that pertain to all subject areas, such as *Assessment* and *Research*.

The *Math* notebook contains workshop notes regarding math teaching strategies, a link to the state's course of study, and a link to the local curriculum guide. A note simply titled "Math Links" includes a list of links to online resources.

Jack wants a way to gather all those notebooks related to curriculum and group them together. He creates a new stack called *Curriculum* and drags each notebook to the stack.

Graduate Studies

Jack started work on his doctorate. He created a stack called *Doctorate*. Each class he takes becomes a notebook within that stack. He also has a notebook in the stack with important emails and announcements regarding the program.

Inside his "Principles of Administration" notebook is a note for each class session. A typical note would include lecture notes, a summary of any class discussion, a PowerPoint presentation or PDF from the professor, or links to resources in Google Slides. If the handout is in paper format, Jack can scan it and drag it into the note. He can also scan a document by taking pictures of the individual pages with his phone. All information for that class meeting lives within that one note.

Current Projects Stack

Separate actionable items from reference material. That concept is important in any workflow. Some information supports a current project. Other information is for reference and is not attached to any project or action.

For that reason, I highly recommend creating a stack called */Current Projects*. Notice the punctuation at the beginning of the stack name. I want that stack to appear just below *.Inbox* and above all other notebooks. Having the "/" does the trick.

Projects tend to generate meeting notes, emails, photos, information from online resources, copies of letters, PowerPoint presentations, and more. Create a notebook for the project and house information related to it there.

As I write this book, I have a notebook in my /Current Projects stack called Get Organized Digitally. Inside that notebook is a note for each chapter. When an idea for the book comes to mind, I have a place to put that idea. Over time, I cut and paste those ideas in a logical order. An outline starts to take shape. Emails to and from the publisher also find their home in this notebook. If someone ever wonders if you can use Evernote to write a book, the answer is, "Yes you can!"

Tags: Return to Grandma's Kitchen

Close your eyes for a moment. Imagine the smells coming from Grandma's kitchen. You probably still remember some of those recipe cards on the counter by the stove.

Each recipe card was like an Evernote note. The file box that housed them was like the notebook. But Grandma did one thing more. Grandma used "tags."

In the upper right corner, she wrote "Chicken" on this card and "Pork" on that one. She wrote "Salad" on this one and "Dessert" on that one. She wrote "Thanksgiving" on some and "Summer" on others. She knew each family member had favorite recipes. That's why some cards said "Timmy" or "Susie" in the corner.

When a holiday approached and she wanted to fix a dessert that Susie would really love, Grandma thumbed through the notecards in the recipe file box. If her search found a card that had "Susie" and "Dessert" and "Thanksgiving" penciled in the corner, her search was successful.

Grandma had a system that worked even though it might have been time-consuming. She did the best she could with what she had. That's the challenge her generation leaves to us...doing the best we can in an age when we have so much more.

Evernote lets us "tag" notes. It's a way to further categorize notes within a notebook. A note can have more than one tag.

Jack's Tagging Strategy

Jack had created a notebook for his children Allison, Jessica, and Zeke. He put them in a stack called Children so they would appear together.

After a while, each of the three notebooks begins to accumulate many notes. Some relate to school. Others relate to visits to the doctor. Still others relate to after-school activities.

Like Grandma, Jack could use some tags. He opens Evernote and clicks on *Tags* in the left-hand pane. A blank list appears in the middle. He clicks on the icon of a tag and keys on a name for his first tag.

"Years from now, I might want to see everything surrounding Jessica's 2nd-grade year," he thought. "I might want to see all of Zeke's medical records or all of Allison's music-related activities."

So, Jack started creating tags. He created one for *1st_Grade*, another for *2nd_grade*, and so forth. He created a tag for *Baseball*, *Basketball*, and *Volleyball*. He created a tag for *Piano*, *Ballet*, and *Scouting*. Jack created a tag for *Doctor* and *Dentist*.

In the left-hand pane, Jack saw an alphabetical list of the tags he created, as illustrated in Figure 5.3.

Jessica needs a physical in order to play little league baseball at the end of her 3rd grade year. Jack creates a note for that doctor visit. He includes information on how much Jessica weighs and enters comments from the doctor. At the bottom of the note, he sees the spot where he can add tags. As he enters text, Evernote suggests already-created tags starting with those letters. Jack tags the note *Doctor*, and *3rd Grade*, and *Baseball*.

Jack finds when he clicks on the *Doctor* tag in the left-hand pane, he sees every note in Evernote with the *Doctor* tag. These notes are not only related to Jessica. Evernote returns any notes tagged *Doctor* for any family

Tags
_____

1^{st}_Grade (14)
2^{nd}_Grade (17)
3^{rd}_Grade (20)
4^{th}_Grade (24)
5^{th}_Grade (12)
6^{th}_Grade (15)
Ballet (4)
Baseball (7)
Basketball (10)
Dentist (4)
Doctor (5)
Piano (9)
Scouting (5)
Volleyball (4)

Figure 5.3 Sample tags

members. Jack also finds he can use the filter at the top of the preview pane to choose any combination of notebooks and tags.

Stacks, Notebooks, Notes, and Tags provide the building blocks of Evernote. Much more could be written about tagging. However, what we have covered will give you a great start. You will be able to create a logical system that lets you store and retrieve the information that is important to you.

Evernote Web Clipper

When we read a magazine in a print edition and come to an article to save, what do we do? Take a pair of scissors and "clip" the article. Hole punch it and put it into a notebook.

The Evernote Web Clipper is the digital equivalent. The Web Clipper is a browser extension. It allows users to take the contents of any webpage and save to Evernote. The content is then editable within Evernote.

Much of our information comes by way of the Internet. When you read an article online and want to save it for future reference, how would you do that? Perhaps you would bookmark the article. Of course, if the author removes that article from its current URL, the bookmark will be no good. How can you take the full text of the article and save it?

Sure, you could click and drag the mouse down the page to highlight the entire thing. Then choose *copy*. Then create a new note in Evernote. Then click in the body of the note and choose *paste*.

Or you could use the Evernote Web Clipper:

1   Click the Web Clipper extension.

2   Click *Save*.

The entire page, complete with formatting, links, images, etc. is now saved as an Evernote note. It shows up in the default notebook (*.Inbox*).

How do you get the Web Clipper? In your browser, go to evernote. com/webclipper and add it as a browser extension. It appears in the toolbar as a small picture of an elephant head.

After installing, open a webpage and click on the Web Clipper. The first time, it will ask for your Evernote username and password. That way, it knows whose Evernote account should receive the information.

My recommendation is to check two settings within the Web Clipper. First, click the gear icon marked *Settings*. On the *General* tab, select that new notes go to a specific notebook: *.Inbox*. You do not want Evernote to use "smart filing." Likewise, uncheck "smart filing" for tag selection. The rest of the default setting will be fine.

Try your hand at clipping the *Article, Simplified article, Full page,* or *Bookmark* to see the difference. Go to *.Inbox* to see the result. Discover how the clipped selection is editable. Add wording, change wording, and manipulate the information as desired.

Exporting Notes from Kindle

Are you someone who enjoys highlighting text in books and writing in the margins? In the physical world, that practice has two drawbacks.

First, it's poor practice for books belonging to someone else. Second, the highlights and notes are all over the place. They are contained in the pages of countless books on many shelves.

What if we could bring those notes together? What if we could highlight in books that do not belong to us without destroying the property of the owner?

Do you read books on Kindle or through the free Kindle app? Go to read.amazon.com/notebook and view the highlights and notes made during your reading. Down the left side of the page are all the titles. Click on one and see the highlights and notes.

But what if that site were to go away? What would happen to the highlights and notes? An easy solution is the Evernote Web Clipper. Each book becomes a note. Create a notebook called something like *Book Notes* and save the clips there. The notes become searchable and shareable. Even if the Kindle service went away, the notes are safe in Evernote.

Forwarding Emails to Evernote

You have seen how to enter information into Evernote in each of the following ways:

- Keying it.
- Snapping a photo.

- Recording audio.
- Dragging information into a note.
- Web Clipping information.

Users on a paid Evernote plan receive a special email address. Any email sent to that address goes into the Evernote *.Inbox.*

I mentioned that one of my personal uses for Evernote is writing this book. I created a notebook for the project and put it into my */Current Projects* stack. When I receive a significant email about the project, I forward it to Evernote and drag the resulting note to the correct notebook. When I send a significant email about this project, I bcc the Evernote address. My email also winds up in Evernote.

We will talk more about this option in Chapter 8 as we explore email.

Saving Time with Templates

Forms help us organize information. Good ones serve as reminders of what to include. They give our information a consistent look. They keep us from "reinventing the wheel" when doing routine things. Think about the forms or templates you currently use or could use in your personal or professional life:

- Meeting planner.
- Packing checklist.
- Lesson plans.
- Project planning.
- Checklist for steps in hiring a teacher.
- Interview form.
- Teacher "checkoff" list.

Evernote provides a *Template Gallery* of premade samples. Paid users can also create and save their own.

When creating a new note, notice the option in the body of the note to use a template. Clicking on the icon opens the *Template Gallery*. Click on one and its contents populate the note. Is the template close to what is needed but requires some modifications? Edit the template and then click the three dots in the upper-right of the note. Choose *Save as template*.

Want to create a template from scratch? Just start a new note. Consider inserting a table. Use the circular *Insert* button at the top of the note. When the template is created, use the three dots in the upper-right corner of the note to *Save as template*.

Where will you find the templates you created? When you start to create a new note, click the *Template* button inside the note. The screen will display the *Template Gallery* of pre-made templates on one tab. *My Templates* displays on a second tab. All users have access to the *Template Gallery*. Only users with paid accounts can save to *My Templates*.

Tagging with Classroom Observations

When Jack visits multiple classes, he creates a single note for that day's visits. He jots a sentence or two about anything of significance. For a more formal information observation, Jack uses a template he created in Evernote.

How can he keep up with who has received a formal observation and who has not? Since he does several observations during the year for each teacher, how can he keep up with who has been left out?

Jack created a tag called *1st_Observation*, one for *2nd_Observation* and one for *3rd_Observation*. Notice the underscore. Creating tag names with no spaces is good practice. It makes more advanced searches possible.

At any point, Jack can click his *Classroom Observations* notebook and scroll through the middle column. He sees a preview of every observation.

What if Jack wants to see the observations for a particular teacher? He puts the name of the teacher in the search window. From the middle column, he uses the filter to select the *Classroom_Observations* notebook.

If Jack wants to see only the first observation for all teachers, he uses a filter. He filters for both the *Classroom_Observations* notebook and *1st_ Observation* tag.

Jack decides to go a step further with his tagging. He wants the ability to view all particularly good visits to any given teacher. Likewise, he would like the ability to see all lessons that were not so good.

In Evernote, he creates five tags: *Excellent, Good, Average, Needs Improvement*, and *Unsatisfactory*. When Jack reviews the notes taken during the day, he adds the appropriate tag to describe the strength of the teaching he observed. Jack could now filter to see such notes as all *1st_ Observation* visits that were also *Excellent*.

Later in the year, suppose Jack wants to see all lessons taught by "Nancy Smith" he described as *Excellent*. He searches Evernote for "Nancy Smith." He filters the search to the *Classroom_Observations* notebook and *Excellent* tag. Jack sees the desired result. He could now change the filter to search for the *Good, Average, Needs Improvement*, or *Unsatisfactory* visits to gain a good perspective of Nancy Smith's overall performance.

Likewise, Jack can search *Classroom_Observations* for all notes tagged as *Excellent*. He would see all visits, regardless of the teacher, representing top-notch teaching. Searching that same notebook for *Unsatisfactory* gives an overall view of the weakest teaching. The title of each note includes the name of the teacher, the date/time, and the subject. Each note includes Jack's text, photographs, and audio notes related to the lesson.

Tagging with Lesson Plans

How could a teacher use Evernote to house lesson plans? How can the teacher access the lesson plans from any computer and any mobile device?

1   Create a stack called *Lesson Plans*.

2   Create a notebook for each subject inside the *Lesson Plans* stack.

3   Create and save a template for the lesson plans.

4   Create a tag for each week (*Week_1, Week_2*, etc.). In all, the teacher would need around 40.

5   Let each lesson plan represent one week of lessons for that subject.

6   The title of the note could reflect the overall topic or could duplicate the name of the subject and week. The teacher has a great deal of flexibility here.

It's now the third week of school. How can the teacher quickly see the lesson plans for this week? In the list of tags, click the *Week_3* tag. The teacher now sees a short list of notes…one for each subject for that week.

Search and Search Syntax

Evernote's search is both intuitive and powerful. Enter a word in the search window and Evernote returns every note containing that word. Evernote even looks for the word inside a picture.

As with searches in most other software, entering two words returns results containing *both* words. Entering *school bus* in the search returns notes that contain both "school" *and* "bus" anywhere in the note. Enclosing the search in quotation marks, such as *"school bus"* causes Evernote to look for an exact phrase.

To further refine a search, after entering a term in the search window, Evernote offers a search filter at the top of the notes list. Filter the search term to only those notes with certain tags, certain notebooks, containing certain elements, created within a certain time frame, or updated within a certain time frame.

Evernote has a powerful search syntax. Here are some of the more common techniques:

intitle:school finds any note where the word *school* is in the title of the note.

-intitle:bus finds any note where *bus* is *not* in the title.

any:school bus driver finds notes that have any of the words. It serves as an "or" search.

tag:math finds all notes tagged *math*.

created:20210701 finds any note created *on or after* July 1, 2021. The format is YYYYMMDD.

updated:20210701 finds any note *updated on or after* July 1, 2021. The format is YYYYMMDD.

created:week Returns notes that were created in this calendar week (Sunday–Saturday).

created:day-1 Matches notes that were created yesterday or today.

created:day-2 will return notes that were created in the last two days.

Advanced users can combine search syntax. As an example, *intitle:school -intitle:bus tag:math created:20210905* would return all notes having "school" in the title but not having "bus" in the title, also tagged "math" and created after September 5, 2021.

Will you need to perform a complex search more than once? Save time by creating a *Saved Search*. Near the top of the *Search results* page, look for the *Save search* link. To access a saved search later, click the search window and they will appear in the list.

For most day-to-day use, using the search window in conjunction with the filter will find what's needed. Advanced users can search for "Evernote Search Syntax" and find the entire list. (Using the Web Clipper to save that page to Evernote would be a good idea.)

Links and Sharing

To this point, we've examined how to get information into Evernote and find what we need via search. We can also share our notes with ourselves, individual friends, or the whole world.

Internal Links

Every note has its own link. In fact, every note has *two* links. Go to any note in your Evernote account and click the three dots in the upper-right corner. On the menu, look for *Copy internal link*. Two choices appear. *Copy web link* copies to the clipboard a link directly to that note.

How could you use this link? In Remember The Milk, we talked about every task having "task notes," and that you could paste a link there.

Jack conducts an observation in Ms. Cook's class. He wants to remember to return after school to discuss the lesson. So, he creates a task in Remember The Milk. He pastes the link in a task note or in the URL field in Remember The Milk. When Jack sees the task this afternoon, putting his hands on the Evernote note requires only one click.

Jack could have pasted that same link in a calendar description. He could also paste a link inside one Evernote note to link it to another.

What about the other link, the one that says *Copy app link*? Later, we discuss the Evernote for Windows and Evernote for Mac software. That app link serves the same purpose. The difference is it opens the note in one of those pieces of software rather than opening it in Evernote Web.

Here is an important point: these two links allow you to view your own Evernote data. You would never give them to someone else. It would do them no good. But what if you want others to have access to something in your account?

Public Links

Jack is presenting at a conference and wants to provide a digital handout for participants. He creates an Evernote note. He places in that note all the information he wants participants to have. How will they be able to see it?

Jack clicks the *Share* button. He flips the *Shareable link* to *Enabled*. What appears is a link he can give to others. Anyone with the link can access the note, just as if it were a link to a webpage. He could email participants and include the link in the body of the email. He could embed the link in a website. He could turn the link into a shortened link using bitly.com or another link shortener.

The news gets better. What if Jack finds a typo five minutes before the presentation starts? He pulls out his phone and opens the note. He fixes the typo. Done! The link stays the same. People viewing the link no longer see the typo.

How do people view the link? Think of it as a link to a webpage. Click the link and view it in the browser. Just like a webpage, there are no page breaks to worry about. The page is responsive and adjusts to the width of the device on which it is being displayed. People can view the page on a computer, tablet, or phone.

What about saving, viewing later, and editing? If a participant is an Evernote user, he/she sees a button: *Save to Evernote*. Evernote saves a copy. The participants can edit the note as desired. Even if Jack deletes the note, the participant still has the annotated copy.

What if someone does not have Evernote? They would treat the link like any other webpage. Here are the options:

- Save the link, such as saving as a bookmark. That option has two downsides. Editing is not possible. Also, if Jack deletes the handout or disables the link, the link no longer works. The upside is if Jack improves the handout, the link always takes the person to the most recent version of the note.

- For Google Keep, download the browser extension for *Save to Google Keep*.

- For Google Drive, download the browser extension for *Save to Drive*.

- For OneNote use the Web Clipper for that platform.

- For Microsoft Word, highlight the entire handout. Copy and paste to a blank document. Editing is now possible.

- Print the handout as PDF, providing a read-only digital copy.

Sharing a Note with an Individual

The same *Share* button that allows making a note public also allows sharing the note with one or more individual people. If those other people are Evernote users, each person can collaborate on the note. The stipulation is that only one person can edit the note at a time.

If the other people are not Evernote users, use the *Share* button to email a copy of the note.

Sharing a Notebook with an Individual

As principal and assistant principal, Jack and Michael share the responsibility for classroom observations. Evernote allows Jack to share the entire notebook with Michael:

- Jack clicks *Notebooks* in the left-hand pane. A list of all notebooks appears.

- Jack finds *Classroom_Observations* and clicks the three dots to the right of it.

- Jack chooses *Share notebook* and enters Michael's email address. Jack chooses the *Can edit* option. Michael can conduct observations and save them in *Classroom_Observations*. They can even collaborate on the same observation as long as they are not both trying to work on the same note at the same time.

Clearing the .Inbox

Your system needs to be as fast as the environment in which you operate. Jack's day is typical of school leaders. He needs to be able to move from one activity to the next and be fully present in the moment for each of them. His system allows him to trap the information. Later in the day, when the dust settles, he reviews the notes he's taken. It's all in one place—the Evernote .*Inbox*.

Some of his notes were taken quickly. He now has the opportunity to make improvements to those notes. He is also looking at those notes with a single question in mind: "What do I need to **do** about the notes I have taken?" With time to reflect on his notes, other ideas may occur to him. Jack adds those thoughts to his notes.

Some notes have events associated with them. Jack enters those events on his calendar and includes a link to the note in Evernote. Likewise, those notes generate "to-dos." Jack puts the to-dos in Remember The Milk. He includes a link back to the Evernote note. His tasks and supporting material are always in close contact.

As Jack examines the notes taken during the day, he concludes by adding any needed tags. He then files each note in the appropriate notebook.

When Jack is finished, the .*Inbox* is empty.

 # Evernote "Free" v. Paid Plans

Our exploration of Evernote has centered around the free version of the software. What does the user get with a paid plan? I see five major advantages:

Access on More Devices

Users of the free plan can access the program from two devices. For all practical purposes, one needs to be Evernote Web and the other needs to be the mobile app on your phone.

Paid plans allow users to sync unlimited devices, such as a tablet in addition to the phone.

Evernote for Windows or Evernote for Mac

The software physically residing on your computer provides some additional advantages. My favorite is a universal keyboard shortcut providing an instant *Quick note* no matter what I am working on. When I am in the middle of something else and an idea occurs, pressing Ctrl + Alt + H (Ctrl + Command + H on the Mac) brings up "Quick note," a notepad in the corner of the screen. The content remains there until I delete it or click to convert it into a note.

A second favorite is the ability to "encrypt" text within a note. Perhaps you have shared a notebook with someone else, but you have some sensitive information even that person should not see. Highlight the text, right-click, and choose *Encrypt selected text*. Supply a password of your choosing and the text is hidden until you click and supply the password to unencrypt. Encrypted text can be unlocked to view on the Web or on mobile versions of Evernote.

More Storage

Both accounts provide unlimited storage. The difference is the amount of data you can add each month. At present, users can add 60MB per month for free. Paid plans allow users to store 10GB for the plan currently called "Evernote Personal" and 20GB per month for the "Evernote Professional" plan. For those entering text only, 60MB is probably enough. Pictures would add to that total more quickly.

Email into Evernote

Paid users have a special email address. To find the address, click your name in the upper-left corner of the Evernote window. Choose *Account Info*. Look for *Email Notes to*. Copy and add that email address to your contacts. Each time you wish to forward an email to Evernote, forward to that address.

Custom Templates

All users have access to the *Template Gallery*. Paid users can create and save their own templates.

That being said, free users have an easy workaround. Create a notebook called *Templates*. Create a template, such as a meeting agenda or lesson plan. Save the template to the newly created *Templates* notebook. When it's time to use that template, open it, click the three dots in the upper-right corner, and choose *Duplicate*. Use the duplicate for your project. Leave the original note, the one in the *Templates* notebook, untouched.

Why Don't They Teach That in School?

Traditionally, schools have done an excellent job of teaching notetaking in a pencil and paper environment. Students have a notebook for each class. Students may start a new page for each class meeting. These concepts transfer well to the digital environment.

How could a college student use Evernote to house class notes?

- Create a stack and name it with the name of the semester.
- Create a notebook for each class. Add each one to the stack.
- Create a note in each notebook with general information. Include the contact information and office hours of the professor, exam dates, and a link to the syllabus.
- At the beginning of each class, create a new note within the appropriate notebook.
- Use the formatting capabilities in the menu bar of the note. They allow you to bullet, number, or outline points.
- If the professor provides a PowerPoint presentation about the material, drag it into the body of the note. Do the same with any PDF.
- Professors are good at giving a heads-up about important information likely to appear on the test. Evernote allows highlighting.

- After class, annotate the notes as needed. Research any information that seemed confusing.

- If two friends are taking the same class, one can create the notebook and "share" it with the other. The only downside is two people cannot edit the same note at the same time (although they can both be in the same notebook at the same time). After class, the two friends compare their versions, edit one of them so it contains all the content, and delete the other. The friends now both have identical copies of the note in their shared notebook.

Of all the concepts in this book, "note taking" is the one most closely related to school days. The notes serve as a way to store knowledge until it's needed on the test. In school, the test is most likely to come on Friday and the student has a good idea about what the questions will be. In life, the test can come at any time. The questions are unknown. We can gift our students the ability to be ready for anything.

Next Steps

Ideas come at the most unlikely of times and places. How confident are you that when ideas come you have a system for trapping them quickly and recalling them at the right moment? That's the challenge, and it comes with practice. Our information is only as good as our ability to find it when we need it.

Review the specific use cases. Develop your own ideas about how your notetaking software will fit into your daily life.

Digital Documents
Retrieval Shouldn't Be a Safari

"I know I saved that," is the mantra of the overwhelmed school leader. Finding it can feel like an African safari. In our digital world, instead of feeling like an episode of "Star Trek," we may feel more like "Lost in Space."

When files are organized, we can see what we have and see what we can discard. We have a better knowledge of resources available to us and no longer recreate things we could have merely repurposed.

These principles yield an organized and easy-to-maintain digital filing structure:

- Work from a clean desktop.
- Establish the services required and define the purposes for each one.
- Create a folder structure across each platform that is as parallel as possible.
- Separate documents that support current projects from those that serve as reference material.
- Establish a place for the most commonly used documents and make them easy to retrieve.
- Provide a "drop spot" for new items until they can be filed.
- Put reminders in the digital task list for documents that need to be updated or accessed at certain points in the year.

DOI: 10.4324/9781003179719-9

Uncluttering the Desktop

Tasha prides herself on saving everything. She saves every memo, every report, and every slide deck she creates or receives. Her computer desktop is "Exhibit A." Why does she have them all there? Tasha's answer is, "So I can find them."

That's the dirty lie we tell ourselves. After a while, it's hard to find anything on that cluttered desktop.

The second part of the answer, spoken in a softer tone is, "I don't know where else to put it." That statement reveals the real problem. She has failed to spend time constructing a good system and making decisions about where items will go.

Tasha opens Google Drive and sees one long list that extends for days. "I just search in that little window for what I need," says Tasha.

A digital filing system should have three components:

1   **Documents**. Reference materials that have no action on them. The aim is to be able to find the item when needed.

2   **Current Projects**. Materials related to current work. Simply looking at this folder provides an overview of "what's on your plate."

3   **Fingertip**. The new items used almost daily. These items need to be easily accessible.

Once the structure for a good digital filing system is in place, what will remain on the desktop? The three folders mentioned plus the recycle bin will be the only items left. Download a file to the desktop and it becomes obvious. Take the needed action and put the document in its permanent home. You never wonder what needs to be handled. If the desktop is clear, the documents are in their proper places. Actions related to them are entered in your digital task list.

 # Establishing Services Needed

I recommend maintaining three services for digital documents:

1 **OneDrive (or iCloud).** These cloud services come with your computer's operating system. They allow files to be accessible from any computer.

2 **Dropbox.** Some may question the need for a second service. I use Dropbox as a place to store those items that are a "work in progress."

3 **Google Drive.** The popularity of Google Drive in education means we receive many digital items in this format. We will be asked to create and share many more. Converting Office files to Google Drive or vice versa is time-consuming. Also, strange formatting can result.

 # Documents

Over the years, computer operating systems have included a main folder intended to serve as the place for the documents you create. At various times, it has been called *Documents, Document Library*, or *My Documents*, depending on the platform and version of the operating system. Currently, OneDrive for Windows and iCloud for Mac serve as the digital parallel for the metal filing cabinet. These files have no action attached to them. They simply need to be organized in order for material to be easy to find.

The first step is one related to paper. Examine the filing system in that metal filing cabinet and clean it up. Get the paper system pristine. Then, create a *parallel* system on the computer. For example, if a science teacher is handed a good lesson plan on photosynthesis, the teacher needs a place in the filing cabinet for it. If the same teacher finds a PowerPoint presentation on photosynthesis, that teacher needs a parallel place in the digital filing system. When the paper and digital filing systems parallel each other, items are easier to file and easier to find.

.Temporary Trash Can

Everyone has items of temporary value. The principal receives a flyer about a workshop. She is inclined to drop it in the trashcan. As soon as she does so, however, someone asks about that workshop. A search through the trashcan ensues.

Create a folder in the digital filing system called .*Temporary Trash Can*. Having a period as the first character causes that folder to sort to the top of the list. Review the contents of the folder periodically. Delete items that are obviously junk. This folder prevents that junk from hanging around in your permanent reference system.

Memos and Letters

We all need a place for routine correspondence, both paper and digital. A letter received as an email attachment is a prime example. The key to finding these documents later is having a good naming convention.

Rename the file with the last name of the person, a hyphen, and several words descriptive of the subject matter.

Should the need arise to retrieve the documents weeks or months later, a consistent naming convention makes retrieval easy.

Memos & Letters can serve as a good miscellaneous folder. We send and receive documents that are not necessarily related to a large project. They don't "fit" in any category. *Memos & Letters* serves as a good catch-all for digital documents we are saving merely for documentation.

Monthly Tickler

Education is a cyclic business. We often need to access and update a document the same time each year. Create a folder called *Monthly Tickler*.

Inside *Monthly Tickler*, create 12 folders labeled with the months of the year. Each file contains the documents that need updating during that month.

For example, a secondary principal might have the subject selection forms in the "March" folder. At the beginning of March, seeing the contents of that folder serves as a reminder to update the forms with the date for the next school year. Opening one of the monthly tickler folders serves as the trigger to examine, update, and print each item in there.

A teacher's August folder might contain the "welcome to my class" letter. It might also include an outline of the presentation for Open House. On August 1, the teacher opens the August folder. Seeing the welcome letter and outline serves as a reminder to update and print these two documents.

An annual holiday production may be part of a teacher's activities each December. An introductory letter about that production is in the October folder. A draft of last year's program is in the November folder. A letter inviting the superintendent to attend the production is also in the November folder. A request for the media to cover the event is found in the same folder. Opening one of the *Monthly tickler* folders serves as the trigger. It reminds the teacher to examine, update, and print each item.

As one example, in the heat of the busy holiday season, how easy would it be to simply forget to drop the superintendent a letter of invitation? Imagine the superintendent being asked about his absence from the program. His reply is he received no information about it. How embarrassing would it be for the teacher when this situation occurs? Having last year's invitation letter in the November file serves as the trigger to send this year's letter.

A two-second date change and execution of the print command is all that is needed to take care of the superintendent's invitation. Hurt feelings and social slights are not necessarily the result of not caring. Instead, they can and do result from caring, yet overwhelmed, people. They lack systems for handling the details.

What keeps you from forgetting to check this *Monthly Tickler*? Create a new task on your digital task list. Call that task, "Check Monthly Tickler on computer." Set a due date. Set the repeating pattern for "Monthly." Once each month, you will be reminded to go to the *Monthly Tickler* and handle each item.

Additional Folder Recommendations

What other folders would you need? Everyone has different needs, but it's helpful to see someone else's system and modify it. What follows is my list of folders and subfolders.

- Curriculum & Instruction
  - Academic Support
  - Accreditation
  - Arts
  - Assessment
  - Athletics
  - Clubs

- Electives
- Federal Programs
- Goals
- Guidance & Counseling
- Language Arts
- Library
- Mathematics
- Physical Education
- Reading
- Scheduling
- School Publications
- Science
- Social Studies
- Special Education
- State Testing Program
- Teaching Strategies
- Technology
- Textbook Selection
- Finance & Budget
  - Budgets
  - Financial Spreadsheets
  - Grant Opportunities
  - Grants Submitted
- General School Management
  - Closing School
  - Emergency Procedures
  - Leadership
  - Maintenance
  - Meeting Notes
- Opening School
- System & School Organization
- Textbooks
- Transportation
- Personnel Management
  - Certification
  - Evaluations
  - Faculty Handbook
  - Hiring
  - Induction
  - Job Descriptions
  - Morale
  - Professional Development
  - Substitutes
  - Termination
- Public Relations
  - Business
  - Community
  - Media
  - Statistics/Issues
- Pupil Personnel Management
  - Attendance
  - Child Nutrition Program
  - Culture and Climate
  - Discipline
  - Grade Reporting
  - Health
  - Parents

- School Law
  - Discipline
  - Curriculum
  - Religion

- Special Education
- Student Rights
- Teacher/Staff Rights

Fingertip Files

Do you have a few files that you use daily or even multiple times during the day? Examples could include:

- School Letterhead
- Memo Template
- Thank-You Note Template
- Master Schedule
- Purchase Order Form
- Financial Spreadsheet
- Expense Form
- Meeting Planner

Keep those often-used items in one folder at your fingertips. You save time not having to navigate through layers of folders. Create a folder within OneDrive or iCloud called *Fingertip Files*. It becomes the one place to house those few files you use constantly.

Create a shortcut to that folder. Move the shortcut to the desktop. Opening one folder from the desktop displays those items you want to have "at your fingertips."

Current Projects

Projects generally have supporting material. The digital task list provides a notes section for each task. We talked about the */Current_Projects* stack in Evernote. It is a place for the notes related to a specific project. Projects don't just generate notes. They also generate documents. We need a parallel place for those digital documents.

For years, I have used Dropbox as this parallel. It's the place to store documents, spreadsheets, presentations, photos, audio files, and video files related to an ongoing project.

Create a folder within Dropbox for each ongoing project. Place the related files into the appropriate folders. Merely opening Dropbox gives me an overview of my current projects and what type of supporting material is available.

Using Dropbox is not a necessity. Creating a *Current Projects* folder within OneDrive or iCloud would work. Create a shortcut to the desktop. Now, all the supporting material for current projects is easy to access.

For me, OneDrive serves as my "digital filing cabinet" for reference information. Dropbox holds supporting material for current projects. That distinction keeps actionable items separate from non-actionable items.

When a project is complete, examine the supporting material in Dropbox. Make decisions on what to delete and what to retain. Next, move the file. I have a folder in OneDrive called *Projects-Complete*. With a good reference system, quality work from years gone by is accessible. Repurposing that quality material saves time. Why constantly reinvent the wheel?

One Example: Handling Digital Photos

One example of this concept is with photos. On my phone, I have the app for both Google Photos and Dropbox. When I take a photo, it uploads to both Google Photos and Dropbox. Google Photos is my main service for organizing photos. However, I want to have a back-up in place if something ever happens.

Every photo goes to a folder in Dropbox called *Camera Uploads*. Just as with documents, photos that have action associated with them live in Dropbox. In this case, the needed action is to periodically clean up and organize the pictures.

The good photos and the duds alike wind up in Dropbox. Every few months, I take time to open that *Camera Uploads* folder. The first order of business is to delete the duds and duplicates. The next step is to create folders for each trip or event represented. Then, we drag the photos to the appropriate folders.

The final step of the process is to drag these newly created folders to a folder in OneDrive called *Pictures*.

Google Drive

Google Drive is ubiquitous in education. Like every school leader, Tasha receives many emails containing links to shared items. Those items live in someone's Google Drive. Likewise, the faculty handbook, student hand-book, and a host of forms and other documents are stored in Google Drive.

Tasha uses Google Drive to create and save many of her own files. The problem was simple. For a long time, she could never find anything. She had some folders, but then much of what she had was a loose list of files. She would scroll for pages to find a needed document. Other times, she would throw a search term in the window and hope for the best.

All the while, Tasha had this nagging feeling she really had a great deal of valuable information in her Google Drive. If only she could organize it, she would have something she could enjoy.

Make the System Parallel

The digital filing system in OneDrive or iCloud should parallel the paper filing system. The system in Google Drive should also parallel the filing system discussed earlier in this chapter.

Google Drive will serve as the *Documents* folder. Inside it, create a *.Temporary Trashcan*, *Memos & Letters* folder, a *Monthly Tickler* folder, and parallels for all other applicable files in your *Documents* folder. If you create or receive a document in Word, Excel, or PowerPoint, for example, you will have a place to put it. If someone shares a Google Drive docu-ment, sheet, or slides file, you will have a place to put it.

"Starred": The Fingertip Files of Google Drive

Files you need "at your fingertips" shouldn't be nested three layers down in a filing system. In Google Drive, one solution is to create a *.Fingertip Files* folder to house those few files that receive constant use. Notice the period at the beginning of the file name. That punctuation causes it to sort to the top of the list of folders.

Google Drive also has a built-in option. Tasha uses a specific spreadsheet to track finances over which she has control. She uses that spreadsheet almost every day. As she started to clean up her Google Drive by making folders, she created one called "Financial." That folder seemed the logical place for her financial spreadsheet. But to put it "at her fingertips," Tasha used a technique she learned: "starring" files or folders.

In Google Drive, Tasha clicked on her financial spreadsheet to highlight it. From the vertical ellipsis (the three vertical dots in the menu), she chooses *Add to Starred*. The file stays in its original folder. But Tasha can click *Starred* in the left-hand menu to see this financial spreadsheet.

Tasha has a copy of the school letterhead saved as a template in Microsoft Word. She keeps it in her *Fingertip File* in OneDrive. Therefore, Tasha also has a copy of the school letterhead saved as a template in Google Drive. She has it in a folder she created called *Templates*. She starred the letterhead. Now it appears in her *Starred* menu.

The caution is not to "star" too many items. Otherwise, the list becomes long and unusable.

Everything Goes in a Folder

We cleared our computer desktop, right? No document gets to live on the desktop. That way, when we download a document to the desktop, it stands out. It's obviously out of place. It serves as a trigger to make decisions about the file name and where to save it.

Parallel that concept in Google Drive. A loose file in Google Drive is a file out of place. This concept not only keeps Google Drive clean, but it also keeps "junk" or poorly named files from becoming part of permanent storage.

Tasha has been trying to master Google Sheets. When she reads an article about a particular Google Sheet technique, she often creates a quick Google Sheet to try the technique hands on. Her idea is to delete that Google Sheet after she practices the technique.

But a principal's day gets busy and we don't always have the ability to tidy up in the moment. Later, Tasha returns to her Google Drive. She sees that lone Google Sheet sitting outside a folder. Seeing a single file is her trigger to make a decision about that Google Sheet. In this case, she will send it to the Trash. Any loose file in Google Drive will represent a decision yet to be made about its title, destination, or usefulness.

"Save to Google Drive" Extension

In Chapter 5, we examined the Evernote Web Clipper. It provides an efficient way to trap content from the Web.

The *Save to Google Drive* Chrome extension is the parallel. It allows saving information from the Web to Google Drive.

After installing the extension, right-click to examine the options. At times, what you want is the image of the page just as it appeared on the Web. If so, select one of the options that saves as a "PNG" file. Other times, you wish to be able to edit the text. If so, choose the "Google Document" option.

The options also ask where to save the clips. Choose *My Drive*. Let's examine the advantage of that option.

Tasha sees an article on the Web she wishes to save in her Google Drive. Her assistant tells her she has a phone call, so Tasha has only a second. She clicks the *Save to Google Drive* extension in her toolbar. She is now free to turn her full attention to the phone call. The system she established in Google Drive gives her the freedom to forget. The next time she opens Google Drive, she sees the lone file sitting outside a folder. That's her trigger to edit the name of the file if needed, edit the text of the clip if needed, and then drag the file to the appropriate folder.

Dealing with "Shared with Me"

One of the common questions among Google users is, "How do I organize the *Shared with me* menu?" The answer is easy: You can't. This list will always be a hodgepodge.

Start by getting rid of the junk. Some items will be of no use. Right-click an item and choose "Remove." To make the process go faster, multi-select items. To do so, hold the *Ctrl* key as you click each file. Click the trash can icon and they are gone.

You have a choice about the remaining items. The owner may be making updates. Since the files are shared with you, you will also see the latest version. That option may be best. However, a downside exists. If the owner decides to delete the file or unshare it, you lose the information.

To be sure you always have access to the file, right-click on it and select *Make a copy*. If the file was called "ABC Report," a file called "Copy of ABC Report" appears as a loose file in Google Drive. This action is the digital parallel of laying a document on a copying machine. The copy is yours. You can annotate it and your changes do not affect the original. Likewise, any changes to the original do not change your copy.

While working through *Shared with me*, it's possible to multi-select items to copy. Hold the *Ctrl* key while clicking each file. Click the vertical ellipsis on the toolbar and choose *Make a copy*. All the copies show up as loose items in Google Drive.

The next time you open Google Drive, seeing those loose items is the trigger to change the title (so it no longer starts with the words "Copy of") and move it to the desired folder. At this point, it's fine to remove those items from *Shared with me*. That action has no effect on the copies made.

If you always want the "latest and greatest" version of a shared file, create a "shortcut." Right-click the item and choose *Add shortcut to Drive*. You can also multi-select items. Hold the *Ctrl* key while clicking each file. Click the vertical ellipsis and choose *Add shortcut to Drive*.

When you open Google Drive, the loose items serve as a trigger to handle them. Move these shortcuts to logical folders. Be sure to leave the original in *Shared with me*, because the shortcut is pointing back to the original from *Shared with me*. When the owner updates the file, it's updated in *Shared with me*. You'll never have to return to *Shared with me*. You'll simply use the shortcut.

What about files that could logically live in more than one folder? Create a shortcut and move that shortcut to the desired folder. Click on a file and use the keyboard shortcut *Shift + Z*. Select the proper destination folder from the menu.

Tasha Cleans Up Her Google Drive

Tasha sets aside a morning to get her Google Drive under control once and for all. She looks at the names of her present folders. She then looks at the naming conventions in her paper filing system and on her OneDrive. She realizes some of her Google Drive folders were named in haste. One-by-one, she right-clicks and chooses to *Rename*.

The next step is to examine the contents of each folder. She sends junk to the trashcan. Other files are in the wrong place. Tasha clicks the arrow point beside *My Drive* to reveal the folders in her system. One by one, she looks at the contents of each folder and starts dragging files to their new homes in the sidebar.

Tasha's third task is to give a home to every file in *My Drive*. Using the list of folders in the sidebar, she starts dragging files to folders.

The fourth task for Tasha is to tackle *Shared with me*. She moves quite a few items to the trash. She makes copies of others and knows those copies are safe in *My Drive*. Tasha then deletes the originals from *Shared with me*.

Now, junk is in the trashcan. She has made copies of the files she wants to save. Only one group of items remains. This group consists of files the owner might update, and Tasha wants to have the latest versions of them. Tasha's fifth step is to select the entire list (*Ctrl + A*) and from the menu chooses to *Add shortcut to Drive*. Now, the only thing in Tasha's *Shared with me* are items she considers both valuable and likely to be updated by the owner.

Before she leaves *Shared with me*, Tasha's sixth step will keep *Shared with me* maintained. She knows new items will accumulate there. Tasha creates a new monthly repeating task in her digital task list. This task instructs her to go to *Shared with me* and sort the list by the "share date." Everything added since she last cleaned up *Shared with me* will be grouped together.

Tasha will delete some items, make copies of others, and make shortcuts for the rest. During the process, Tasha will come across files such as those shared with her at a convention. While she saved them, she had no trigger to remind her to reread, annotate, or begin using the contents. That repeating task put the new items front and center.

Tasha realizes the value of putting reminders to read items in her digital task list. She copies the link to any such document and pastes it into a task. Tasha rests assured her system will remind her to review the material at the right time.

For step seven, Tasha returns to *My Drive*. Earlier, she took care of the loose files and put everything into a folder. Now, the copies and shortcuts she made earlier all sit loose. She moves each of these items to the appropriate folder.

Moving to step eight, Tasha notices two areas where titles need changes. First, she sees titles beginning with the words "Copy of…" Those words are unnecessary. Tasha goes to the search window and clicks the drop-down arrow to reveal all the search options. In the *Item name* field, she enters. "Copy of" and clicks *Search*. Every item needing that title change appears. Tasha works through the whole list and removes the words "Copy of" from the title.

Tasha also notices some items have the title "Untitled." She searches the *Item name* field for the word "untitled." The search returns every file that had been inadvertently saved without a title. Tasha starts fixing them one by one.

Link to It

We never know when we will need a piece of information or a document. A good filing system makes it easy to find when we need it.

Other times, we know when we will need that information or document. For example, Tasha will meet with the Strategic Planning Committee two weeks from now. She already knows of three documents she wants to have at hand. Every digital note or digital document has a unique URL. She will use this capability to make retrieval effortless.

As Tasha plans, she copies the URLs for the documents needed for the meeting two weeks away. She opens the event on her calendar and adds the links into the description of the meeting.

Tasha uses her digital task list as the tool that drives her daily actions. Completing those actions often means consulting supporting information. Tasha copies links to that supporting material and pastes them into the appropriate tasks. When it's time to do the task, Tasha is a click away from the supporting material.

Why Don't They Teach That in School?

Today's students create digital documents on a daily basis. Like the locker, the bookbag, or the three-ring binder, the collection of digital documents is a mess for many students.

Creating a logical filing system is a skill that must be taught. Just like the locker, bookbag, or three-ring binder, keeping a digital filing system clean requires some time. However, the effort is worth it. The dividends it pays include allowing students to be able to find their best work months or years later.

The blank page is a curse for the writer. When a student possesses a personal knowledge library made up of digital notes and digital documents, he or she rarely sees a blank page. That young person is always able to call on past knowledge and use it to create something new and better.

Next Steps

Your digital information is only as good as your ability to find it when you need it. Our digital storage systems provide an unlimited capacity to store information. They also provide unlimited places to lose it. When we don't know what we have or cannot find it, we might as well not have it. Invest a little time in a filing system that works the same, regardless of the medium. That investment pays dividends every day.

Rounding Out Your Digital Treasure Chest

The Digital Calendar
Building and Sharing Your Day

The calendar is, without a doubt, the most-used time management tool in modern society. Students become familiar with the monthly grid in kindergarten and depend on this friend throughout life. For centuries, the calendar has helped people show up at the right place at the right time.

However, our digital world presents challenges those who went before us did not have. Luckily, we also have digital tools to meet those challenges. Learning the basics of a digital calendar is easy. In this chapter you'll learn the basics and a good bit more.

 ## Calendars Then and Now

The most basic calendar management can be summarized in three rules:

1 Have a calendar.

2 Have only *one* calendar. The person who has two calendars cannot trust either.

3 Put all appointments on the calendar. Get rid of random scraps of paper and reliance on memory.

We've seen people who had a large desk calendar, a paper planner, a wall calendar, and a small pocket calendar. It's no wonder they never seem to know where they are supposed to be.

DOI: 10.4324/9781003179719-11

Rise of the Digital Calendar

When the desktop computer began to become a mainstay in the workplace, some of the first software allowed executives to keep their calendar on the computer. The programs offered impressive advantages:

1   Repeating events could be added once. They would show up each week, month, year, or at other intervals.

2   When an event changed, no erasing, striking through, or rewriting was required. A few keystrokes moved the event to the new date.

3   The calendar could be viewed in a monthly grid, a weekly table, or a daily list.

Those digital calendars had one problem. The information was on the computer only. Walking away from the computer also meant walking away from the calendar. Paper planners, such as Day-Timer and Franklin continued to be the go-to time management solutions.

Introduction of the Mobile Device

The Palm Pilot released in 1996. Busy professionals could have a digital calendar on the computer that would synchronize with a digital calendar on the mobile device. The same software and device also allowed for a digital address book, to-do list, and notes.

BlackBerry released in 1999 and took the business world by storm. The device that housed the calendar, contacts, tasks, and notes added the ability to handle email and allow phone calls.

Apple's iPhone revolutionized mobile devices in 2007. It offered a computer in your pocket with a wide variety of third-party apps. It brought syncing through "the cloud" to the average person. A change made on the computer's calendar updated the event on the mobile device without the user having to perform a manual sync.

A year later, Android entered the picture. Google supplied the software. A number of manufacturers created hardware to run that software.

What Is Easy Gets Done

The story of the mobile device is a story about making technology access-ible. When the digital calendar becomes easier than its paper-based coun-terpart, people will use a digital calendar.

The story of mobile devices is also a story of difficult entry. Those who remember the Palm also remember the special stylus and the required spe-cial type of alphabet, known as "Graffiti." Mastering Graffiti came with a learning curve.

The BlackBerry introduced a miniature keyboard. The iPhone introduced the concept of typing with two thumbs on a piece of glass. Input has always been the Achilles' heel of the mobile device.

Voice input has moved input from being hard to input being easier than paper. Siri for iOS and Google Assistant for Android allow us to add to our calendars vocally. We can even ask those services for a verbal readout of what's on our calendar for the current day.

The potential is there for technology to do the heavy lifting. As a result, we can spend more time perfecting our craft of teaching and learning. However, we have a challenge. We've got to learn how to use the tools.

How do you know if you're using technology correctly? If it's easy, that's a good sign it's correct.

New Demands on an Old Tool

Our grandparents wrote appointments on their calendars. They hand-copied items from newspapers or letters and wrote them in their calendars. They negotiated appointments on the phone or in person and wrote the resulting appointments on their calendars.

Today, emails embed dates for our calendars. Those same emails also include details about the event. Websites alert us of events and the many details that surround them.

In generations past, a telephone appointment would also have a phone number penciled in the calendar beside the name. Today, that appointment needs to have a long URL to log into a video conference.

These new demands, coupled with powerful tools to meet them, pro-vide the reason so many of us keep our calendars digitally.

Why "Put It on Your Calendar" Doesn't Work

A common piece of advice people give is, "Put it all on your calendar." The idea is, "What's on your calendar gets done." Those people say put appointments, holidays, and events on the calendar. They say put all the to-dos on the calendar. They say to put when you're going to eat lunch and when you'll exercise and when you'll brush your teeth on the calendar.

That advice has its share of problems.

1   **Most of what we have to do doesn't have to be done on a particular day at a particular time**. Therefore, the calendar becomes a mix of true appointments and arbitrary to-dos. With such an arrangement, seeing the true appointment becomes more difficult. "Put it all on your calendar" leads to a very cluttered calendar.

2   **Anything not accomplished today must be moved manually**. Unlike the task list, the calendar lacks a way to "check things off." Day after day, we drag unfinished items to arbitrary days and arbitrary times.

3   **The monthly view becomes useless**. The monthly calendar view is a fantastic tool for seeing the big picture. However, any square can only display a handful of items. Trying to cram everything into the calendar makes the calendar unreadable.

4   **It's hard to give a "yes" or "no" answer**. When an opportunity presents itself and we're asked if we are available, we need to be able to answer. With to-dos on the calendar, we must wade through the clutter to find the ones that truly represent appointments we must honor.

5   **You can never use your automated scheduler**. Whenever someone goes to the link you provide, all days for the foreseeable future appear to be booked to capacity. In reality, some of those days may not have included a single true appointment.

There's a better way to use the calendar. My calendar tells me where I am. And it tells me the specific things I want to know about that day.

My task list shows me the to-dos that at some time in the past I wanted to see today. And it shows me the to-dos from yesterday that didn't get done. They roll over without me doing a thing.

Calendar Sharing: The Baileys' Story

William and Maria Bailey work in the same school district. William is in his first year as a middle school assistant principal. Maria holds the same position in the elementary school across town. They have three children. Eric is 13, Cindy is 7, and Bobby just turned 2.

William and Maria always thought of themselves as organized people. But things were falling through the cracks. Both William and Maria lived by their paper planners. A calendar on the refrigerator held appointments for each family member, at least in theory.

In practice, the commitments for the Baily household were scattered all over several calendars, a school-issued assignment book, and random papers relegated to the bottom of book bags. Details for appointments were trapped in emails. On the weekend, William and Maria would compare planners and conduct a scavenger hunt in an attempt to figure out what the week ahead would hold. It all seemed to take too much time and was frustrating for every family member.

Sharing Google Calendars

Through this chapter, we will focus on Google Calendar because of its popularity, power, and simplicity.

William and Maria both have Google accounts. Therefore, they both also have Google calendars. They started brainstorming their family needs. Appointments happening during the workday would not need to be shared with each other. Appointments related to parent conferences and teacher observations the other was conducting would only serve to clutter the spouse's calendar.

The critical items to share with each other were after-school, evening, and weekend appointments. So, William and Maria decided the default calendar for each would be their work calendars. Each created a calendar in the left sidebar of their respective calendars. They named the calendars *William Personal* and *Maria Personal* respectively. Each clicked the ellipsis beside the calendar name to select the *settings & sharing* for the calendar.

Under *Share with specific people*, each added the other person and granted rights to make changes to events. With sharing in place, William could look at his Google Calendar and see three distinct calendars. He would see his work calendar (for which he chose a blue color), his personal calendar (in red), and Maria's personal calendar (in purple). Things were already looking better!

Maria liked to plan surprises. She worried how she would keep the plans for William's surprise party from him now that they had shared calendars. Maria noticed when she opened an appointment, she could click a dropdown labeled *Default visibility* and change it to *Private*.

William and Maria looked back at their paper planners and realized they often entered events for information only. They lived in a college town, and traffic was always heavy on fall Saturdays when the football game was at home. Cultural events were plentiful in their town.

Maria went into Google Calendar and added another calendar. She called it *FYI* and chose a bright yellow for its color. She shared it with William. They pulled the various flyers off the refrigerator door and started entering events of interest into the *FYI* calendar. One click on any event opened it and allowed the couple to enter details and an address for any event.

What About the Children?

Three children kept the "Bailey Bus" busy. Keeping up with soccer practice and band events for Eric, soccer and dance for Cindy, and medical appointments for all three children was a never-ending struggle.

Eric had gotten a phone for his birthday. William and Maria decided it was time to put the phone to work. Eric had a Google account. Therefore, he had a Google Calendar. The couple showed Eric how to share the calendar with each of them and give them rights to add events.

One of the family struggles had been getting Eric to write his events on the "refrigerator calendar." He would forget. Even when he remembered, mom and dad would forget to look at the refrigerator. When you're a school administrator, it's embarrassing to get a call from the soccer coach to tell you everyone has been picked up from practice...except *your* child!

Eric quickly adopted the habit of adding appointments to his calendar. Like magic, they appeared for both William and Maria in a green color. Eric learned how to add to his calendar with his voice. That capability made adding to his calendar even easier and more fun.

Eric had a big smile on his face when the dental assistant handed him a card for his next appointment. He whipped out his phone and said,

"OK Google, add Dental Appointment to my calendar December 19th at 2PM." As he put his phone back in his pocket, the dental assistant couldn't help but be impressed. No longer did the Bailey family need little cards magnetized to the refrigerator. They faithfully used their calendars.

Eric added practices and games and concerts. The Symphonic Band trumpets had after-school sectional rehearsals every Tuesday afternoon. Eric added the event once and clicked for it to repeat every week at the same time.

He put his parents' birthdays and their anniversary on his calendar and made those repeating annual events. Like his mother, Eric found how he could make an event *Private* and not show up on his parents' calendars. Suddenly, forgetful Eric was remembering those special days. William and Maria were wondering what happened to this "boy of theirs."

Eric added school projects, church events, and major tests. Nightly interrogations from mom and dad became a thing of the past. The conversation at family mealtime became less about the mechanics of events and more about the successes of the day. That phone Eric got for his birthday was now beginning to earn its keep.

William and Maria felt Cindy was a little young to manage her own events. So, William went to his Google Calendar and created one more, an orange calendar for Cindy, her favorite color. He shared the calendar with Maria and gave her edit rights. He also created a brown-colored calendar for two-year-old Bobby. Mother and father could each see a calendar for every member of the family and turn any calendar on or off. They could see the calendar displayed as a month, a week, or a day. They could see the calendar from their desktop computer, laptop, tablet, or phone.

Who's Driving the "Bailey Bus"?

Knowing where each child was supposed to be and when simplified life for William and Maria. But a question mark remained. Who would provide transportation for each child? Eric was responsible for negotiating transportation and being sure the appropriate parent had entered it on their calendar. If he was riding his bike or riding with a friend's parent, he was responsible for updating the appointment in his calendar to reflect that.

As for Cindy and Bobby, if Maria was going to be responsible for transportation, she would click the appointment, change the calendar for that event to her own calendar, and save. William would do likewise. If an upcoming appointment was still showing in Cindy's color or Bobby's color, that meant William and Maria needed to decide who would be responsible for transportation.

Notifications

William asked, "Maria, when I look at my calendar, I can see your events. But I find myself looking weeks into the future to see you have added something new. Is there any way when you add something to your calendar, you could tell me or email me, or something?"

Maria did a little research and came up with an answer. She had William go into the "settings" for each calendar and look for *Other notifications*. Here, William could choose to get an email when an event was added, changed, or canceled from that calendar. Maria did the same for calendars shared with her. As soon as Eric added an extra band practice to his calendar, both William and Maria got an email. When William's evening graduate class was moved an hour later, as soon as he made the change on his calendar, Maria received an email.

Speaking of notifications, William, Maria, and Eric began to reap another benefit. Fifteen minutes before any calendar event, the phone would vibrate and an audible reminder would sound. In the Bailey household, forgetting became a thing of the past.

Calendar Subscriptions

We've seen how we can add to our calendars and see the calendars shared with us. "Subscribing" to a calendar allows events to populate automatically. If the event changes, the change automatically updates on the calendar of anyone who subscribed to that calendar.

In the left-hand pane, look at the *Other calendars* section and click the "plus" sign to add other calendars. *Browse calendars of interest* allows for the addition of holidays, moon phases, or schedules from sports teams.

Does your school or church have a Google Calendar embedded on its website? If so, look at the lower-right corner of that calendar and find

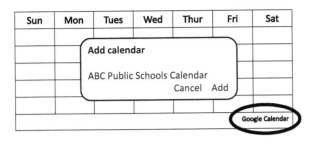

Figure 7.1 Subscribing to an embedded Google Calendar

Figure 7.2 Making a Google Calendar available to the public

a seemingly insignificant label that says, "Google Calendar," as shown in Figure 7.1. Click it. A message appears providing an opportunity to add that calendar. Accept and all events from that calendar are added to your calendar in its own color. If changes are made to the calendar, the change updates on your calendar.

A coach could create a calendar for practices and another for games. In the settings for each calendar, the coach would check the box for *Make available to public* and *Get shareable link* (Figure 7.2). The coach would give those links to the players. When a player goes to that link, the calendar appears with the option to "add" to the student's calendar. The coach could embed either calendar on a team website and allow others to click the lower right corner and subscribe. The coach could also send the link to the principal and other interested faculty members.

The school's administrative assistant could maintain a master calendar for the entire school. The assistant would simply gather all the shareable links for all the sporting or club events created within the school. The assistant could then embed that master calendar on a school website. Those viewing the master calendar could turn on and off any calendars.

Calendar Invitations

William started to learn more about the capabilities of Google Calendar. One of the features cut down on the emails he was sending and the confusion his staff was experiencing.

When William scheduled a faculty meeting or committee meeting, he would send an email with the date, time, and location. Several days before the meeting, he would email an agenda. It was common to resend updated agendas and email attachments so everyone would have the needed documents. Sometimes, the meeting had to be rescheduled. William would send another email with the new information.

45 Teachers Were Overwhelmed

When 45 faculty members received an email announcing a faculty meeting, 45 teachers went to 45 calendars to mechanically enter the meeting. Any change meant 45 teachers would go back to 45 calendars to make 45 changes in the date, time, or location.

Then, an email would arrive with the agenda, and 45 teachers would wrestle with what to do with that email so that on the day and time of the faculty meeting, each person would have that agenda. Organizing the documents which came as email attachments presented another challenge.

Some frustrated teachers would arrive at the meeting with stacks of paper. Others would arrive with no papers, but the reason was because they missed the email with the attachments.

45 Teachers Found Peace of Mind

William's readings led him to a discussion of "calendar invitations." Now, when he schedules a meeting, he merely puts it on his own calendar. As for the agenda and attachments, William includes them as part of the appointment.

William's school uses both Zoom (zoom.us) and Google Meet (meet. google.com) for many of its conferences. William noticed a button

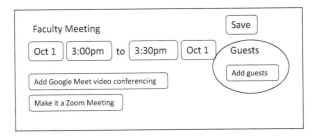

Figure 7.3 Sending calendar invitations

within each calendar event. With one click, that button would make the meeting a Google Meet event. William learned he could install a Chrome extension providing a similar button to make a meeting a Zoom session (Figure 7.3).

After entering the event on his own calendar, he included the "guests" to invite, a field he found in each meeting. Since he already had the entire faculty as a group in his contacts, he saw that same group as an option when inviting someone to the meeting.

Now, 45 teachers automatically received an email letting them know about the meeting and asking if they would attend. Clicking "Yes" put the meeting on the teacher's calendar. Inside that meeting was all the information and any attachments.

At William's end, he could see who had accepted the invitations and could follow up with others as needed. If William needed to add to the agenda, he simply made the addition in his own Google Calendar. The same applied for adding another attachment or even making a change to the date or time. Teachers received a notification via email of the change. But 45 teachers no longer had to make 45 changes to 45 calendars. Google Calendar made all the changes.

When it's time for the meeting, teachers don't need to search through emails to find the agenda or attachments. Click the event in the calendar and it's all there. If the meeting is via videoconference, there's no need to search through emails for the link. It's all there in the calendar event.

Throughout the history of education, schools have delegated many clerical duties to teachers. Once upon a time, that was the best we could do. Technology gives us the ability to change that. Vision makes it reality.

Webinar Invitations

William and Maria enjoy the professional development opportunities coming their way through free webinars. Gone are the days when they would register and then carefully enter the event, date, time, and URL into their calendars. Now, they just look for the hyperlink to "add to calendar" and click it. All the information is on their calendars and the time zone adjustments are handled for them. When it's time for the webinar to begin, they're not hunting for an email. The links to join are already within the events on their calendars.

Automated Schedulers: The End of Email Battleship

One of the time bandits and frustrations for the school leader is scheduling meetings or phone calls. You fire off an email, "Can we get together to talk about the budget? How's Tuesday at 9:00 for you?"

A few hours later, the return message says, "I'm booked then. How's Wednesday at 1:00?"

You respond, "Not good for me. Any chance of doing Thursday at either 9:00 or 3:00?"

The following morning, the other person replies, "Sorry, no luck on either of those."

It's like playing a game of "Battleship" by email. Each person is trying for a "hit" on a calendar that can't be seen.

Next comes the "heavy artillery": "Let's try for the next week. I have Monday at 9:00, 10:30, and 4:00. Tuesday is good from 9:00 all the way through 3:00. Wednesday, I'm free from 8:00 to 10:00."

Three days later when the other person finally replies, the time slot picked is the one single option that has now been gobbled-up by something else. Back to "square one"! And so it goes…back and forth, back and forth.

What If It Was as Easy as Clicking a Link?

If the problem is trying to hit a calendar you can't see, perhaps the answer is being able to see the calendar. Or, at least, what if we could see the times the other person is available? That's the idea behind automated scheduling software. They put a stop to "Email Battleship." As this book goes to press, the simplest and the one I recommend is Calendly.

Creating a Calendly Account

Go to Calendly.com and create a free account. All automated schedulers have common elements. You'll grant permission for Calendly to view your main Google Calendar. It knows when you are free and when you already have an appointment.

Next, you'll be able to establish some rules. What's the earliest time you would like someone to be able to schedule an appointment with you? What's the latest time? Perhaps you only want Calendly to allow scheduling appointments with you in the afternoon and perhaps only on certain days of the week. You'll give Calendly that information just once.

Calendly provides a link for you to give to others. They click the link and can see when you're available. The other person does not see what your events are. All they see are the times you're available.

They choose a time. The choice goes on *your* calendar. The choice goes on *their* calendar. The calendar event holds the relevant information: the person's name, phone number, email address, and comments they made. If you like, a setting in Calendly will create a Zoom meeting and give the login information to both you and the other person. You also receive an email alerting you about a new appointment. Calendly even allows for a reminder email to go to the other person.

But Be Careful

Think of that link the way you think of your personal mobile phone number. In fact, it's even more treasured. Don't put it in your email signature or on the school website. If that happens, your calendar is not your own. Never offer your time carte blanche for anyone to grab for free.

Who gets the link? For starters, give it to your administrative assistant, who will know when you are booked and when you are free. Other members of the administrative team need the link. Your superintendent needs the link. This one technique will save telephone tag and back-and-forth emails.

That link will come in handy. Read how Maria made her month of May much calmer.

Ending Maria's May Madness

Each spring, Maria was responsible for being part of the Individualized Education Program (IEP) team for special education students. In addition to IEP meetings, Maria and her principal met with each non-tenured teacher for an end-of-year evaluation.

As special education teachers were scheduling IEP meetings, they somehow needed to know when Maria was available. In the past, the school had no good way of doing that. This year, Maria gave the special education teachers her Calendly link. She also gave the link to the teachers who needed to schedule conferences with her. She added the stipulation that the link was only to be used for these specific purposes. It wasn't intended for an "open season" on her calendar all year long.

Each day, Maria's email would include notifications letting her know what had been added to her calendar, all within the rules she had created in Calendly. Maria retained total control over her calendar and had the peace of mind that nothing was falling through the cracks.

Ad Hoc Meetings with Chrome Extension

Maria often receives an email from a parent asking for a meeting. In the past, that sort of email would signal the beginning of "Email Battleship." Trying to schedule the meeting with a phone call usually ended up in telephone tag.

Maria added a Calendly Chrome extension. When she clicked to reply to an email, Maria would see a small Calendly icon at the bottom of the email message. Clicking it allowed her to select an "Ad Hoc Meeting." A copy of Maria's calendar filled the screen, letting her view what she had scheduled and what was free. Maria could begin to click on different times she had available and wanted to offer to the parent.

Calendly inserted all these times into the email. When the parent received the email response, all he/she had to do was click on a time. The selection, along with all the needed information, went on Maria's calendar and then the parent's calendar.

Google "Appointment Slots"

Those with Google for Education accounts can allow others to book appointments through a feature called "Appointment Slots." Start by creating a calendar event as normal in Google Calendar. Select the date. Choose a start time and end time for the block to be devoted to appointments. Will these same appointment slots be needed on a regular basis, such as each week on the same day? If so, make the appointment a repeating event.

Within the event, click the "Appointment slots" button and choose the desired duration. Next, save the event.

How will people sign up for appointments? They will need a link. Open the event and click "Go to appointment page for this calendar link." Copy the link on the page which appears and make that link available to others. When someone signs up for a timeslot, the results appear on the owner's calendar.

Doodle: When You Need to Schedule the Whole Group

Calendly is for scheduling one-on-one meetings. The goal is to find a time when two people can meet. What about those times when the goal is to find a time when half a dozen people are all free?

Doodle.com is an old favorite for this purpose and is free. Select some options for a day and time for the meeting. Add the people to be invited. Each person will indicate all the times he/she is available. The meeting organizer looks at the results and makes a choice based on the feedback in Doodle.

The Superintendent Calls

When William and Maria were both summoned to the superintendent's office, they were a little nervous.

"This Calendly thing," he began. "It works well for you?" The couple explained a little more about it and how it integrated with their Google Calendars. They also explained the other ways a digital calendar had made their lives easier.

"Is this something you could teach our other administrators?" he asked. "It just seems we have too many little pieces of paper flying around and too many dropped balls. We have a team meeting in three weeks and I would like the two of you to be the feature."

And So They Planned...

After dinner, William and Maria sat down at the kitchen table. Maria booted her laptop and began typing... "Advantages of a digital calendar." They started to brainstorm. And here is what they listed:

- **Saves money**. Google Calendar is free and powerful enough to handle all your needs.

- **Enter repeating events once**. Think of how many events happen every week or every month at the same time. With a digital calendar, enter the event once and decide when it repeats.

- **No mess**. Plans change. Drag the event to the new date. No more strikethroughs.

- **Room for details**. The large block holds all the information about the event. View the agenda for the meeting, who will be in attendance, questions to ask, and even attachments for needed documents. Add the location. When it's time to leave, Google Maps is ready to give you turn-by-turn directions.

- **View in a variety of ways**. Some people like to see the "big picture" and opt for a month-at-a-glance calendar. Others want to see one day at a time. With a digital calendar, we can have our cake and eat it too. One tap or keystroke toggles between the month, the week, and the day.

- **Share calendars**. Say goodbye to synchronizing paper calendars. See as many calendars as needed all at once. Toggle some on or off for focus.

- **Subscribe to other calendars.** You don't have to key anything.

- **It's always with you**. If you've got your phone, you have your calendar. No more having to get back to someone after you check your calendar.

- **It reminds you**. The phone vibrates and dings when the appointment is nearing. A notice pops up on your computer screen. When days get busy, the digital calendar never forgets where your attention needs to be.

- **No more "Email Battleship"!** Scheduling with others is so much easier.

- **Add with your voice.** Entering information on a mobile device can be awkward. Voice input makes it easy.

- **Your calendar "goes that far."** How many times do you hear someone say they can't book a future date because "…my calendar doesn't go that far"? A digital calendar never runs out.

And that's what *you* can also have with a digital calendar.

 # Why Don't They Teach That in School?

Students need a way to see the "big picture." How many weeks is it until spring break? How many weeks until the term paper is due or the class takes that big field trip? How many days are left before basketball tryouts?

Initially, a paper calendar is a great tool, and school assignment books provide that structure. Building the habit of recording events in that planner can be built starting in 1st grade.

Calculators are plentiful, but we first teach students manual computation. Once a student masters the concepts, a calculator provides speed and lessens careless errors.

By the same token, a digital calendar should never substitute for the ability to manage a calendar. We must teach students to trap appointments as soon as they arise. No more relying on memory. The digital calendar adds the speed and convenience discussed in this chapter. Students using Google Classroom will see assignments appearing on their own Google Calendars. They can see the "big picture" plus all the steps along the way.

Next Steps

Start with your own implementation of a digital calendar. Expand outward to include your closest co-workers, such as the administrative staff and front office.

Success at work makes success at home easier and vice versa. Discuss with your spouse or significant other how the family can use a digital calendar. You can have every event that applies to you, any family member, or your school at a glance. You can have it anywhere in any number of views. When your faculty understands how easy having it all in one place can be, they can have it too.

Email Mastery
The Hub of Your
Communication

Email gets a bad rap, and it's a shame. Used correctly, email is an efficient form of written communication. The reader composes it at a time when it's convenient. The recipient reads it at a time when it's convenient. But somehow it's become the enemy, and the overflowing inbox causes stress levels to rise.

How did we get in this mess? How do we get out of it? This chapter is about making email a friend.

The Crazy Neighbor

Imagine the house across the street from you sold and the new neighbors moved in. The next day, you notice your neighbor walk to the mailbox, take out the mail, read it while standing at the mailbox, and then put the mail back in the mailbox.

The next day, you witness the same scenario. The neighbor is not confused as to which is the new mail. It's the mail on the top of the stack. After a week, the mail carrier can barely fit another piece of mail into that overstuffed mailbox.

When asked why he keeps all of his mail in the mailbox, he replies, "That way, I know where it is."

We would never do something so crazy with the mailbox in front of our houses. We empty it every day. We make decisions about what each piece of mail means to us. Bills to pay go one place. Magazines to read go somewhere else. Junk goes in the trashcan. It's all about little decisions.

DOI: 10.4324/9781003179719-12

While we would never allow mail to accumulate in that metal mailbox by the road, that's exactly how most people handle the email inbox on their computers.

The Decisions We Make

Every email falls into one of six categories:

1   A place to be.

2   A thing to do.

3   Good reference information.

4   Documentation "just in case."

5   A task to delegate.

6   Junk.

Watch as Melanie shows Savannah how to make the decisions that will get the inbox empty every day. The example we use will be primarily Gmail with some references to Microsoft Outlook. Regardless of the platform, every email in the inbox represents a decision yet to be made.

Savannah's Out-of-Control Email

"Don't get me wrong; I love my job. But email is eating me alive." Those were the words of first-year principal Savannah to her mentor, Melanie. Every Saturday morning, the two met at a local coffee shop. On this particular Saturday, Savannah was feeling especially overwhelmed.

"Twelve thousand," said Savannah. "Twelve thousand emails. That's what was in my email inbox when I left yesterday. I hardly know what I've handled and what I haven't. I feel like things are slipping through the cracks, especially when people call me on the phone saying I haven't responded to their emails. I try to just search for what I need, but it's just all a mess."

Melanie remembered having been in that same situation a few years earlier. So, she knew what it took to dig out of that hole and how to stay on top of email.

"We're going to your office," said Melanie. When we leave, you won't have those 12,000 emails in your inbox. In fact, you won't even have 12. Savannah could hardly believe her ears.

A Place to Be: Put It on the Calendar

The two colleagues arrived at Savannah's office, booted the computer, and began the quest to tame the email inbox.

Melanie began, "Let's look through these first couple of screens and see if we can find an email related to **a place you need to be**." Savannah scrolled a few screens and found the perfect example.

"Here's an email from our superintendent about the retreat next month," remarked Savannah. "I'm saving it because it has all the information about the address, the time we start, what to bring, the full agenda, and even parking information."

"That's all well and good," replied Melanie. "But you just had to scroll through seven screens to find it. By next month, I can only imagine how far down the list it will be."

"When an email relates to a *place you need to be*, a better place for this information would be on your *calendar*." Melanie clicks the vertical ellipsis and chooses *Create event*. A box opens—it's a new Google Calendar event. The subject of the email appears as the name of the event. The body of the email appears in the event description.

Melanie continues, "You can edit the name of the event if needed. Enter a date and time. Save it and it's on your *calendar*. On the day of the event, the address, agenda, parking information, and all the rest is right there…on your *calendar*. Now, you can either delete or archive the email. Either way, you now have one less email in your inbox."

Outlook users have the ability to "drag and drop." Click on the email and drag it to the *Calendar* button. Outlook opens a new appointment. The subject of the email automatically populates the subject line of the appointment. The body of the email is displayed in the notes section of the appointment. Set the date and time. Save the appointment. Now, either delete or archive the email.

After reading about digital calendars in Chapter 7, you might wonder why the superintendent didn't simply send this information as a *calendar invitation* instead of an email. The calendar invitation would have been a more efficient option and would have saved each recipient from having to manually enter information on calendars and manually update as details change.

Melanie sat patiently as Savannah scrolled through more screens to find appointments disguised as emails. One by one, she clicked the vertical ellipsis to turn them into calendar appointments.

A Thing to Do: Put It on the Task List

Melanie proceeded to the next topic, "Now let's see if we can find an email that is sitting in your inbox because it's a reminder of something *you need to do.*"

"That's easy," Savannah said with a laugh. "I have tons of them. Here's one—another email from the superintendent. He needs a budget proposal for our music program. That's going to take me some time to do, so it's sitting here as a reminder."

"Savannah, you had to scroll two screens to even see it! How in the world do you call that a *reminder?*"

"That's sort of my problem," Savannah responded with a sigh.

"If the email is something you can handle quickly, go ahead and handle it right then. You have already read it and done some thinking about it, so don't waste that time. Do it and be done with it." Melanie continued, "But if you can't do it right then, put it on your digital task list. Decide when you want to see that task again and assign a due date that makes it happen."

Earlier, we discussed the seven essential elements to look for when choosing a digital task list. One of those elements is the ability to communicate with email. Savannah went back into Remember The Milk, found her secret email address, and created a contact for it.

As Melanie watched, Savannah hit *forward* on the email, entered the Remember The Milk email address, edited the subject line so it reflected exactly what Savannah needed to do, added the due date as part of the subject, and hit *send.*

"You just earned the right to forget about that task," remarked Melanie. "On the day you designated, that task is going to show up on your list. All the detail from the body of the email will be in the notes section of the task. Now, you can either delete or archive the email."

Savannah started scrolling from screen to screen identifying tasks embedded in email. For each one, she hit *forward*, entered the Remember The Milk email address, edited the subject line, and sent the email.

Long-time Outlook users may know about the ability to click an email and drag it to the "Task" button. Outlook creates a new task. The subject of the email becomes the subject line of the task, but the user can edit it. The body of the email appears in the notes section of the task, which the user can also edit.

Savannah started to feel the days of scrolling through pages of emails and things slipping through the cracks were about to end. Her appointments are on her calendar. Her to-dos are in her digital task list.

But she still has plenty of email in her inbox.

Good Reference Information: Forward to Evernote

Melanie started to laugh. "Look at that email at the bottom of the page! It's a chocolate chip cookie recipe from one of your teachers."

"She makes the *best* cookies," Savannah remarked. "I want to hang onto that recipe."

"It's great you want to keep it. But email is a terrible place to do it. That recipe is an example of *reference information*. Forward that email to your secret Evernote email address. The next time you open Evernote, you'll see that recipe. Put it in the correct notebook. You are done with having to scroll through screen after screen of emails to find your favorite recipes. When you forward the email to Evernote, you can delete or archive the email."

The special Evernote email address is only open to users of the paid account. All users, both paid and free, have access to a free Evernote for Gmail add-on. After installing, the add-on appears in the right-hand side panel of Gmail.

OneNote users also have an email address to forward emails to OneNote. Those who would store something like this recipe in Google Drive can go to the Chrome Store and add the *Save to Google Drive* extension. This extension works much like the Evernote Web Clipper. Clicking the *Save to Google Drive* extension saves the contents there. The next time the user opens Google Drive, this new document will be obvious, because it will be loose and not in a folder.

Finally, the user could export the email as a PDF and save it in any folder in OneDrive, iCloud, or Dropbox. To create this PDF, select the *print* option. In the box that allows the user to select which printer to use, an option will appear to *Print to PDF*.

"Let me make a suggestion," Melanie interjected. "It's going to take you a while to scroll back through all these emails and forward reference information to Evernote. Create a new Remember The Milk task telling you to work through email and find the reference information. Let's move on to the next type of email you have. You still have thousands of emails in your inbox. Why?"

Documentation: Archive It

Savannah sighed, "Well, I don't know when I may need some of these again. I mean, I get emails from parents and I have returned their emails and handled what needed to be handled. But I just feel like I need to hang onto those emails just in case something comes up."

"So, in other words, you're talking about documentation," said Melanie. Documentation is good, and email makes it easy. The problem is the inbox is the wrong place to keep it. You're about to have a much better place for all this documentation."

Melanie led Savannah through the following steps:

1   While looking at the list of emails in the inbox, place a check in the box at the very top of the list. All emails on that page become checked.

2   Look for a message asking whether the action will apply to only the emails on that page or to all emails in the inbox. Select the option to let the action apply to all emails.

3   On the menu bar at the top, find the *Archive* button and click it.

"Let's give Gmail a minute to work its magic," said Melanie with a smile.

Email Is Empty

A couple of minutes passed. Nothing happened. Savannah thought something might be wrong.

Suddenly, all the emails vanished. Her inbox was empty.

"Oh my! What happened?" exclaimed Savannah. "Where did my emails go?"

"Relax. *Archive* moves the emails out of your inbox. In the left-hand pane, click on *All Mail*." It's all there. When you need to find an email you saved for documentation purposes, click *All Mail* and search for it there. When you're finished, click back on the inbox."

You no doubt know people who have created an array of folders down the left-hand side of the screen. They diligently drag emails one at a time to folders labeled with names of people, projects, or subjects. The practice is a hold-over from paper filing systems, and it's totally unnecessary,

We've identified actions on the front end and forwarded email messages to the calendar, task list, or notes program. Most of what we archive we will never need again. Dragging each email to a folder is not only time-consuming, but it invites error. A misfiled message is a lost message. *Archive* and then use Gmail's powerful search capabilities to find information.

Outlook users have much the same capability. Work through emails from the last several weeks. Determine those to drag to the calendar, those to drag to the task list, and those to forward to wherever reference information is being kept.

To archive everything else, click the first email, scroll to the bottom of the list, hold the *Shift* key, and click the last email. All emails in between will highlight. Click the *Archive* button in the menu.

Working Through All Mail

Savannah reached a major milestone—an empty inbox, and she did it in one sitting. She does have a big "to-do" on her task list. She did not have time to go through the entire inbox to find all the "reference" emails, emails such as the chocolate chip cookie recipe. She likely has good information going back several years that she has totally forgotten about because it's been in a hodgepodge of messages. She has a task on her list to work through the list.

During her cleanup of *All Mail*, Savannah will find three categories:

1   Reference information. As we stated, she will forward those emails to Evernote. (Other users would forward to OneNote, use the *Save to Google Drive* extension, or *Print to PDP*.)

2 Documentation. These emails have no action on them. Most will never be needed again. Leave them alone.

3 Junk. When Savannah archived her inbox, that action included many archived emails she knows for sure will never be of any value. As she reviews her *All Mail* at her leisure, Savannah will delete them.

Delegation, Follow-up, and Follow-through

Melanie asked Savannah to click one more email menu item: *Sent*. As they scrolled through the list, they saw emails where Savannah asked for information or delegated tasks to someone else.

"How do you keep up with whether or not other people respond to your email or do what you asked them to do?" was Melanie's question.

"Good question," responded Savannah. "I wish I knew."

Savannah has learned the hard way that others often drop the ball. But she has never found a way to keep up with what she is expecting to receive from others. She has no way to follow up on those items where someone else is responsible. The "dropped balls" often make Savannah look bad.

Melanie could see Savannah was perplexed on this one. "I have an easy way to handle this type of situation. When you delegate by email, you can *bcc* your special Remember The Milk email address. That action creates a task for you. The entire body of the email will be in the notes section of the task and it will be date and time-stamped."

"When you see the task in your Remember The Milk inbox, edit the task line to be sure you include the name of the person. Add a due date and priority. Add *ETR* in the line to show it's something you "expect to receive" from someone else. On the day you wanted to be reminded to follow up, the task will be waiting for you on your list."

Decisions, Decisions

Getting email empty is about making decisions. Make little decisions about what each message represents. Put that message in the right place. Rinse and repeat.

Every email represents either a place to be, a thing to do, reference information to file, documentation to archive, a delegated item to track, or junk to throw away. Whether you use Gmail, Outlook, Apple Mail, or anything else, the principles are the same.

Every email in the inbox represents a decision you have yet to make. Get started on those decisions today.

Favorite Gmail Tricks

Getting email empty is a good trick in itself. What follows are a host of others designed to make email a friend.

Priority Inbox: The Good Stuff Rises to the Top

By default, Gmail separates email into a set of tabs: *Primary, Social, Promotions, Updates,* and *Forums.* That arrangement means getting the inbox empty involves having to look at five different places. A better choice is *Priority Inbox.*

Click the cog in the upper right corner. Scroll down to the *Inbox Type* section and choose *Priority Inbox.* Emails Gmail deems more important appear at the top. Everything else appears below. Gmail makes those decisions based on such criteria as whether you are the lone recipient versus an email being sent to hundreds of other people, whether the sender is someone in your contacts, and whether this is someone whose emails you have answered before.

Gmail does a good job, but you can train it to do even better. Notice the five-sided arrow beside each email. Clicking it toggles the shape between being clear and being solid yellow. Solid yellow represents *Important* emails. If Gmail puts a message in the *Important* section that isn't important, click the arrow to turn it clear. Gmail puts messages from that sender in the *Everything Else* tab from then on.

On the other hand, Gmail will likely put newsletters in the *Everything Else* category, but you may be a fan of a particular one. Click the arrow to turn it solid yellow and Gmail will place it in the *Important* section going forward.

Outlook offers a similar option. At the top of the inbox, look for buttons that say *Focused* and *Other*. The *Focused* inbox is the equivalent of *Important* in Gmail. If Outlook puts a message in the wrong inbox, right-click on the message and choose *Move to Other* or *Move to Focused*. Over time, Outlook will become more accurate.

Auto-advance

By default, after deleting or archiving an email, Gmail returns to the email list. The user must click on another email to read anything else. If that's your desire, fine. But if you would like to go straight from one email to the next straight down the page, turn on *Auto-advance*. Click the cog and choose *See all settings*. Scroll down the *General* tab and find *Auto-advance* and select *Go to the previous (older) conversation*. Now you can go straight through the inbox handling one email after another.

Send and Archive

After replying to an email, the most common thing to do is *Archive* it. Gmail allows you to handle both functions with one click.

On the *General* tab, scroll to *Send and Archive* and select to show that button. When you reply to an email, two buttons appear at the bottom. One lets you send. The original email remains in the inbox so you can take another action on it, such as creating a calendar event, forwarding to the task list, or forwarding to Evernote. The other button sends the reply and archives the original message.

Smart Compose

Turn on all the elements related to this option. While composing the message, watch Gmail suggest the next several words. Hitting *Tab* accepts those suggestions. If the suggestion is not the desired one, continue to type.

For years, I have advocated composing emails by adding the attachments to an email first. That practice prevents you from forgetting to add the attachment. Next, compose the message. Start with the most important information first and include details towards the end. People have short attention spans.

The next thing I have taught is to add the subject. Step back and write a subject line that accurately tells the reader what the message is about and what is expected from the reader. *Smart Compose* will compose the subject line for you, and it's surprisingly good at it,

The Entire General Tab

When we learn a new piece of software, we often learn a few needed elements to get us by and never learn the other capabilities beyond that. Take a moment to explore all the options in the *General* tab.

Ever discover an embarrassing typo just after hitting send? *Undo Send* will allow that email to be recalled up to 30 seconds later. Be sure to turn it on.

Most every Gmail user has experience clicking a star beside an email. Clicking the star toggles between solid and clear. Gmail allows a dozen stars or other icons of various colors. Look for *Stars* on the *General* tab. Drag the stars in the desired order. A yellow star might mean to read the email again. A red star could indicate an email where you are expecting to receive a reply. A yellow exclamation could mark an email as urgent. While I don't have the need, people who insist on leaving emails in the inbox may find this one a lifesaver.

Be sure to turn on *Keyboard shortcuts*. The ones I use most are *C* to compose a new message, *F* to forward, *R* to reply, *E* to archive, and *Z* to undo a mistake. *J* and *K* move to the next and previous messages, respectively. *J* and *K* also have that same function on Google Calendar, Google Contacts, and throughout Google Drive. To see all keyboard shortcuts, while in Gmail, hold *Shift* and hit the question mark.

Scrolling down the page is a place for the signature. You also learn how to compose those out-of-office autoreplies.

Choose a Theme You Love

Click the cog and scroll to the *Themes* section. Clicking *View all* shows a host of options as well as allowing you to upload your own. One of the nice things about getting your email empty is that you are left with that beautiful family picture adorning the entire screen.

Get Good at Search

Everyone knows about the search window at the top of the Gmail screen. We all know about the little search window. Few people click the arrow point at the right-hand end of the window to reveal the search criteria.

How much information do you know about the message you're trying to find? Sometimes, we remember a certain uncommon word or phrase used in the message. Add it to the search. Maybe we have a general idea of when we sent or received the email. The search allows narrowing the search by time frame. If the desired message has an attachment, check that box. Finally, click the drop-down to widen or narrow where Gmail will look. Is the email going to be in the inbox? Searching *All mail* returns the archived emails. For the broadest search, choose *Mail & Spam & Trash*. Combining elements in the search terms reduces what could have been a list three screens long to a mere handful of messages.

Snooze

The *Snooze* icon looks like a clock. It is present at the top of each email. Want to wait and handle a certain type of email all in one batch? Snoozing the message removes it from the inbox and returns it on the right day and time. Want to snooze several emails to the same day and time all at once? While looking at the list of messages, check the box beside each desired one. Right-click and choose *Snooze*.

Send Later

This concept is huge for the school leader who likes to handle email late at night. No principal expects teachers to respond to an email at midnight. Few expect teachers to handle work email on the weekends. We send email at weird times because those times may be convenient for us. Others can respond when it's convenient for them. That's the beauty of email. Yet some people feel the pressure to respond to the boss immediately.

Solve the problem with *Send Later*. Notice the *Send* button in Gmail has a downward arrow. Click it and schedule a date and time to send.

Adding a "+" to Your Gmail Address

Suppose your address is yourname@gmail.com. Following your name, add a plus sign and any text you want. Gmail will still deliver it. Gmail pays no attention to the plus sign or anything after. It delivers it to me. So, yourname+anything@gmail.com shows up in your inbox.

Another example is a teacher who is assigning several accounts in a particular piece of software. Each account needs a unique email address. The teacher could create 20 different accounts and use address myclass+demo1@gmail.com, myclass+demo2@gmail.com, myclass+demo3@gmailcom, etc.

This technique is especially helpful when creating filters. In Chapter 9, read about how Melanie and Savannah use it to manage a poetry contest.

Every Email Has Its Own URL

In Chapter 2, we talked about the convenience of pasting a link in the notes section of a task. When it's time to do the task, click the link, and the supporting information is there. In some cases, the link is to a website containing useful information needed to complete the task.

In Chapter 5, we explored how every note in Evernote has its own link. Paste that link into the description of a calendar appointment or paste it into the notes section of a task. The reference information from Evernote is only a click away.

That same concept extends to Gmail. Open a Gmail message and notice the URL in the address bar. That URL is specific to that email. This concept is huge.

How many times are you planning a conversation and will need to have access to one or more emails at that time? How do you handle that situation? Print the emails and have them on your desk? Copy and paste the body of the messages into the calendar description for that event?

Gmail offers a much easier solution. Melanie receives an email from a parent about her child being bullied. She decides to phone the parent.

Melanie picks up the phone but does not get an answer. She creates a new task in Remember The Milk: *Call Mrs. Jones.* She includes the phone number. She highlights and copies the URL for the email and pastes it in the task. She can put it in the URL field or in the notes section. She adds a date and priority. Melanie archives the email and has now earned the right to forget about that phone call and email. When she sees the task on the list at the appropriate time, she has the phone number in front of her. When the parent answers the phone, Melanie clicks the link to open the archived email.

Conversation View

Click the cog in Gmail and scroll down to *Conversation View*. Place a check in the box. The option is also available in the Gmail *Settings* on the *General* tab.

Think of times when an email has gone back and forth between you and someone else. They respond to your question. You then respond with a couple of your own. If *Conversation View* is on, all of those emails stay together. Often, a principal sends one email to a dozen different teachers asking for feedback on a topic. If *Conversation View* is on, the principal sees those responses together rather than being spread out all over the inbox. Some people love *Conversation View*; others hate it.

For me, the advantage is simple. The entire conversation retains the same URL as the original message. As long as nobody changes the subject line, the same URL is good throughout. Let's revisit Melanie and her email from the parent.

During their phone conversation, they agree to talk again a week later. They also agree to keep each other updated via email throughout the week. Melanie will let the mother know about the actions she is taking and ask the mother for additional input. Mrs. Jones will email Melanie about what she is seeing at home.

Melanie creates a task in Remember The Milk to call Mrs. Jones and gives it a date for one week later. She pastes the URL for the email into the task.

As the two email each other, Melanie does not have to do anything to keep up with the emails back and forth, thanks to *Conversation View*. The one email she already pasted in the task pulls up the entire conversation.

The Dreaded "Thanks"

The emails between Melanie and Mrs. Jones resemble a game of ping-pong as they go back and forth. When Melanie hits *Send*, the entire conversation goes to her *Sent* items. Melanie can also retrieve the conversation from *All Mail*. When Mrs. Jones replies, Melanie finds the conversation in her inbox.

Back and forth that conversation goes between *Sent* and *Inbox*. After Melanie and Mrs. Jones talk by phone, Melanie sends one last email summing up the situation. Mrs. Jones responds with a single word: "Thanks."

Melanie sees the one-word response. Yes, it serves as confirmation that Mrs. Jones read that final message. But it's not something she needs to save.

So, Melanie deletes the "Thanks" email. That's her mistake! Two months later, she wants to review the conversation. She searches *All Mail* to no avail. The conversation is gone.

Here is what happened: When Melanie deleted the "Thanks" email, she also deleted the entire conversation. What she should have done was to archive the "Thanks" email. That action would have archived the entire conversation.

The moral of the story is simple. When in doubt, archive rather than delete.

Making Email a Friend Again

Email is the most efficient form of written communication we have. We can email when it's convenient for us and let the other person respond when it's convenient for them. That way, we can stop interrupting each other so much.

It's easy to save for documentation purposes and searchable for easy retrieval. Its URL lets us link action items to the supporting information in emails.

With a little automation magic, we can make email the hub of our communication. But that's another story for another chapter.

Do Unto Others

The "Golden Rule" applies to email. As school leaders, we dread the overflowing inbox. Think about the teachers and parents with whom you interact. They share those same feelings.

If I am a parent at your school, how many different places do I need to look to stay abreast of what I need to know? Do I need to check the school's Facebook page and Twitter account and Instagram and regularly visit the school's website?

Parents in Melanie's school know they only have to look in one place—the email inbox. Parents can count on one email every Friday afternoon. In fact, the one week Melanie neglected to send it, several parents called just to make sure Melanie was OK.

That weekly email contains all the calendar events, announcements, and celebrations. Sure, the school has social media accounts. Even organizations within the school have accounts. Melanie's weekly email often mentions them and links to them.

However, parents find if they simply read Melanie's weekly email, they never miss a thing. Many parents save those emails and refer back to them throughout the year. It's the "one-stop shop." They depend on it.

Services such as Smore (smore.com), Constant Contact (constantcontact. com), or Mailchimp (mailchimp.com) are perfect for sending a school newsletter via email. Reports let you know who has and has not opened the emails and what links are getting clicks. The newsletter provides an easy archive of the school's news.

Encourage the local media, elected officials, and business leaders to subscribe to the school's newsletter. Let the school's good news reach community leaders through the one tool everyone uses and everyone checks—their email.

As a word of caution, do not try sending to large numbers of people through a regular email message. Doing so is a quick way to hurt your email reputation, have your messages wind up in spam, and even find your email address blacklisted. Use a service designed for sending mass emails.

Why Don't They Teach That in School?

When it comes to email, we don't teach email management because most of us still haven't figured it out. Young people do not want to learn email management from someone who has 50,000 messages in an inbox and no idea what's in any of them. This chapter aims to change that scenario.

Next Steps

Getting email empty is about having places to put each type of email. Each message goes either to the calendar, task list, digital notes, digital documents, email archives, or trash. Making decisions about each email message is the secret to mastering this valuable tool.

Reread the chapter to get a good understanding of how to handle each type of email. Next, set aside a time to get email empty. The good news is you don't need to sort through 50,000 emails. Work through what has come in over the last several days and archive the rest. The inbox is empty. Take your time to work through the archived email. Decide what to trash. Decide what may be valuable reference information to store as a digital note or digital document.

Work through the "Favorite Gmail Tricks" section one trick at a time. Don't leave it to your memory. Create a task in your digital task list for each trick and add a date when you want to review it. Your task list will remind you to keep coming back to this chapter to put in place each one.

Digital Automation
Letting Tech Shoulder the Load

Earlier chapters have given a system to organize each of the following:

1   Things you have to do.

2   Places you need to be.

3   Notes that put important information at your fingertips.

4   Documents that comprise a digital filing cabinet.

5   Incoming information via email.

 ## The Stories We've Shared

The beauty of a digital system is how technology can do the repetitive manual entry. Through the stories in these chapters, you have already seen some examples of digital automation.

Never Recopy a To-Do List Again

Chapters 1–3 showed the simplicity of digital tasks. Enter a task into a digital list and it stays there until it is completed or deleted. What does not get done today rolls over to tomorrow. When the task is completed, Remember The Milk records the date and time, providing an accurate work record.

Repeated tasks need never be re-entered. Each one reappears on the correct day. The capabilities of voice entry mean tasks need not be manually entered at all.

DOI: 10.4324/9781003179719-13

Take Notes Without Keying a Thing

Chapters 4–5 highlight the importance of the microphone key on the phone's keyboard. Use it to trap entire paragraphs with ease by speaking them into the phone. Since our phones are always with us, we are ready when great ideas come to mind.

Use the Evernote Web Clipper to take information from the Internet and import into Evernote with the click of a button. Forward emails into Evernote.

Export Kindle notes and have all notes from all books in one spot. Share notebooks with someone else with whom you collaborate on information. You can store tons of information in Evernote without manually keying a thing.

Let Approved People Add to Your Calendar

Chapter 7 illustrated how technology can maintain our calendars within the parameters we set. Sharing calendars with family members keeps everyone on the same page without manual entry. Designating repeating events prevents lots of manual entry. It also prevents missing a regular appointment because you "just knew" you could remember.

Sending calendar invitations rather than emails reduces errors and saves time for those who plan meetings and those who attend them. When a notification or webinar invitations shows up, look for the link that adds the event to your calendar.

I find when I create a hotel or airline reservation through Gmail, that reservation appears automatically on my Google calendar. As one tip, I would suggest using your Gmail address as the one the hotel chains and airlines have on file.

Use an Appointment Scheduler

Create a Calendly account at Calendly.com. Give your scheduling link to a small circle of trusted people. Give it to larger group but with some strict parameters as to when they can use it. Your time must remain your own, so never allow carte blanche access to your calendar.

Use the Calendly extension for Chrome to schedule ad hoc meetings via email. Eliminate the need for back-and-forth emails as you try to find a convenient time for both parties.

Get Email Empty by Sending It Somewhere Else

A digital system allows the parts to work together. In Chapter 8, you saw a system for sending email to Google Calendar, Remember The Milk, and Evernote. Artificial Intelligence (AI) groups important emails together and helps compose new messages and subject lines.

In this chapter, we look at additional techniques for automating routine procedures. In some cases, automation will handle the task. In other cases, automation will consolidate information so we don't have so many places to look.

If This Then That (IFTTT)

If This Then That (ifttt.com) is a service that allows two or more Web services to work together. More often than not, people refer to it by its acronym, pronounced like "gift" without he "g." The easiest way to explain IFTTT is through examples. With it, the user can have each of these actions and many more:

What if you could put some of those tasks on "autopilot"? Here are some examples:

- If the time is 6:00AM, then send a weather report for the day to my email.

- If I post to Instagram and tag the image with our school hashtag, then post the image and caption also to Twitter and/or Facebook.

- If one of my scheduled blog posts appears, then post an update on Facebook and/or Twitter.

- If one of my scheduled blog posts appears, then update Twitter.

- If the time is 7:00AM on a weekday, then call my elderly mother's phone (even a landline) to wake her up.

- If my favorite college (or pro) sports team scores, then text me.

- If I get an email with an attachment, then make a copy of that attachment in Dropbox.
- If I make or receive a call on my mobile phone, then log the call in a spreadsheet.

Each of these examples has four parts:

- **If**. The beginning of the trigger.
- **This**. A service and condition (Example: Instagram could be the service. The condition could be the creation of a post using the school hashtag.)
- **Then**. The beginning of the action to take.
- **That**. A service and an action (Example: On Twitter, create a post.)

Go to IFTTT.com and create a free account. The service operates through "applets." A free account allows the user to explore any applets in their library and add more. As of the date this book goes to press, users may create up to three applets of their own. With the paid account (currently $3.99 per month), a user may create an unlimited number of applets.

Creating applets is surprisingly easy:

1   Click the *Create* button.
2   A highlighted button appears that says *If This*. Clicking that button is all the user can do.
3   A list of services appears. Click the one that will serve as the trigger (such as *Instagram*).
4   The first time that particular service is being used, IFTTT asks for account information and permissions.
5   A set of conditions appears. In the case of Instagram, the applet can fire for any of the following conditions: *Any new photo by you*, *New photo by you with a specific hashtag*, *Any new video by you*, or *Any video by you with a specific hashtag*. Choose the appropriate one.
6   A highlighted button appears that says *Then That*. Clicking the button is the only choice.

7 A list of services appears. Click the one that will perform the desired action. Again, the first time a service is used, IFTTT will ask for account information and permissions.

8 A set of choices appears. For example, choosing Twitter would allow for these choices: *Post a tweet*, *Post a tweet with image*, *Update profile picture*, or *Update bio*.

9 A box appears allowing the user to add any text as well as add or edit fields.

10 Click the *Create action* button.

11 Click *Continue*.

12 Click *Finish*.

An applet such as this would take only a couple of minutes to create. What follows are some of my favorite IFTTT applets.

Send Important Tweets to Remember The Milk

Reading through Twitter is something I like to do during spare minutes. When standing in the grocery store line, reading tweets from educators is a better use of my time than browsing the tabloids. But what about those tweets that link to a good article? How can I get back to that tweet later when I have more time to digest the article?

I "like" the tweet and keep scrolling through the feed. When I review Remember The Milk, I see a task which reads, "Read this liked tweet" (Figure 9.1). It has a due date of *Today* and is marked *No Priority* so I see

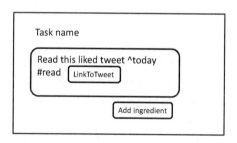

Figure 9.1 Sending "liked" tweet to task list

it in the evening. It's tagged *Read* and therefore appears with other things I wanted to read that evening. The notes section of the task has a link to the original tweet.

How does this piece of magic happen? A simple IFTTT applet says, "If on Twitter I like a tweet, then on Remember The Milk, create a new task."

Add Appointments for Today to My Task List

People often ask about being able to see calendar events and tasks all in the same place. They generally want to know how to get tasks to show up on the calendar. My feeling is having tasks on the calendar causes clutter and prevents seeing events. However, being able to see appointments and tasks together is a worthy idea. I like to go the other way…to have appointments show up on Remember The Milk along with my tasks.

In *If This Then That*, create an applet. Use Google Calendar as the trigger. Several options appear. The one I selected is to have the applet fire 45 minutes before a Google Calendar appointment. The action is to create a task in Remember The Milk with a date of *Today* and a *Priority 1* (Figure 9.2).

Forty-five minutes before the appointment, that appointment pops in at the top of the list in Remember The Milk where I can't miss it. Fifteen minutes before the appointment, Google Calendar gives me a reminder. Five minutes before the appointment, not only does Google Calendar give me another reminder, but Remember The Milk *also* provides one. That reminder sounds like a cowbell! It really gets my attention. There's no way I can forget an appointment.

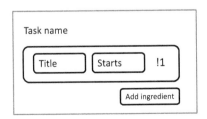

Figure 9.2 Calendar event automatically drops into task list

Create a Running Log in Evernote

Would you like to run a time log throughout the day to see where your time goes? Maybe you want a quick way to jot one-sentence notes about the day.

Suppose I am at a conference and run into Scott, an acquaintance I haven't seen in years. It's nice to have a quick way to jot that piece of information. It's as easy as taking out the phone and saying, "OK, Google, Frank's Journal. Saw Scott Wright at NAESP conference."

In Evernote, one of the notebooks is called *Journal* and one of the notes in it is titled *Frank's Journal*. An IFTTT applet appends "Saw Scott Wright at NAESP conference" to the bottom of the note. It automatically adds a date and time stamp. When I open that note and scroll to the bottom, I see the entry (Figure 9.3).

How does this magic happen? In IFTTT, the trigger is *Google Assistant*. Of the several choices, the one to select is *Say a phrase with a text ingredient*. This IFTTT applet uses Google Assistant and Evernote.

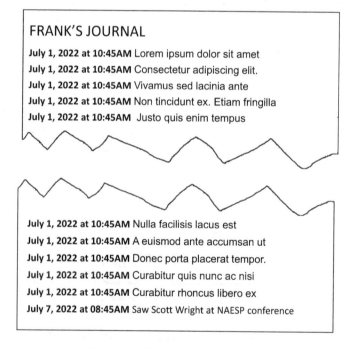

FRANK'S JOURNAL

July 1, 2022 at 10:45AM Lorem ipsum dolor sit amet
July 1, 2022 at 10:45AM Consectetur adipiscing elit.
July 1, 2022 at 10:45AM Vivamus sed lacinia ante
July 1, 2022 at 10:45AM Non tincidunt ex. Etiam fringilla
July 1, 2022 at 10:45AM Justo quis enim tempus

July 1, 2022 at 10:45AM Nulla facilisis lacus est
July 1, 2022 at 10:45AM A euismod ante accumsan ut
July 1, 2022 at 10:45AM Donec porta placerat tempor.
July 1, 2022 at 10:45AM Curabitur quis nunc ac nisi
July 1, 2022 at 10:45AM Curabitur rhoncus libero ex
July 7, 2022 at 08:45AM Saw Scott Wright at NAESP conference

Figure 9.3 Running log in Evernote

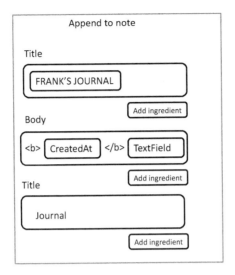

Figure 9.4 How to create log applet

The instructions tell me to enter the phrase I want to serve as the trigger ("Frank's Journal"). I am to follow it with a dollar sign to represent the variable (seeing Scott Wright).

The action part of the applet is Evernote. Of the several choices, one is to "append a note." The applet asks for the notebook name and title of the desired note. Clicking the Add ingredient button allows adding the creation date and time. IFTTT even allows some HTML code. I choose to bold the date and time (Figure 9.4).

Before Evernote, recording these moments in my life would mean logging them in a paper journal. Using this little piece of automation means all I need to log the events of the day are the phone and my voice.

As one can imagine, this *Frank's Journal* note would grow in length over time. At the end of each month, I create a new note in the Journal notebook and name it for that month and year. I then cut and paste everything from the *Frank's Journal* note into this newly created note. *Frank's Journal* is ready for the next month, and I have a searchable log of the little happenings of my days.

What if you like this idea but are using different equipment or software? Try the same thing with another smart speaker or voice input service. For example, instead of using Evernote, a Google Sheet could serve as the log. Each entry would be a new line. The first cell in each line could be the date and time stamp.

Send Text Messages to Email

Personally, I don't care for text messaging. It's one more place to have to look. Email is my hub of communication. The more communication I can funnel to email instead of having to check other places, the happier I am.

I use a very simple IFTTT applet that says, "If I receive an SMS message, then use Gmail to send myself a message." Sure, I reply to the text message with the text app. But what about any follow-up or to-do associated with the text? That's the beauty of having this information not only in the text message but also in an email message. I can now use the email message to create an event in Google Calendar, a task in Remember The Milk, or a note in Evernote. I can archive it, and it becomes searchable through Gmail's powerful search features.

Voice Mail: It's Not 1984 Anymore

The blinking light is so attractive, isn't it? Be it the phone on your credenza or the phone in your pocket, the curiosity to see "who it is" is alluring. We listen to it and promise ourselves we will go back later and get the details. But life happens, we forget, and we beat ourselves up for letting yet one more thing slip through the cracks. End the madness by making it a rule to handle each message exactly one time.

Have a tool at hand to trap the information. For many decades, that tool would have been a paper notepad and pen. For today's Evernote user, the tool could be pressing Ctrl + Alt + H (Ctrl + Command + N on Mac). This simple keyboard shortcut brings up a digital notepad in the corner of the screen. The advantage of the digital method is the ability to copy and paste that information into tasks on the digital task list.

In any case, ignore the blinking light until the time is right. Then, trap it all in your system. Get the name, the number, and the message. Funnel everything you need to do into the task list.

With your present phone system, do you have a way to transcribe voice mail? Will that text show up in your email? If so, the need to take notes from the voice mail message goes away. Copy and paste the transcription where it needs to go. Imagine creating a task to return a call to "Joe" and being able to paste a text transcription of his voice-mail message into the notes section of the task.

Google Voice (voice.google.com) transcribes voice mail for me. This free service provides its own phone number. Google Voice allows that number to ring any or all your phones just by associating those phone numbers with it. In the Google Voice settings, choose to have messages transcribed and emailed.

Want to decrease the number of messages you receive and increase the quality? Put your outgoing message to work. My outgoing greeting in 1984 gave callers a mini lesson in how the technology worked. It told the caller I wasn't there, something they probably figured out, and how I would call them "as soon as possible." Exactly what does "as soon as possible mean"?

Later in my career, my message became more helpful to the caller. It also made my like easier: "Hello, this is Frank Buck. I generally return calls between 3:30 and 4:00. Please leave me your name, a number where I can reach you at that time, and a detailed message so I can prepare for our call."

That short message communicates several points:

1   **Don't sit by the phone expecting a return call in the next five minutes**. The call is going to come between 3:30 and 4:00.

2   **There's no need to call back and leave more messages**. It won't help. The call will come between 3:30 and 4:00.

3   **Be reachable between 3:30 and 4:00**, because your phone will ring. This one is important. Always do what you say you'll do.

4   **The call needs to have a focus**. Let me know what we're going to be talking about and I will be prepared. That one phrase, "… detailed message, so I can prepare for our call" saves me from being blindsided. It gives me the gift of time to research the situation and be prepared. It keeps me from being turned into merely a listener who ends the conversation with "I will look into this and get back to you."

Feedly: For the Blogs You Love

Blogs provide a great way to stay on top of what's happening and what's of interest. The problem becomes one of *time*. Visiting multiple blogs to see if new content has posted is time-consuming and inefficient. You identify more and more good blogs. You then spend more and more time going to each one to read new content.

What if you could go to one place and see the new posts from all your favorite blogs? What if you could dismiss the posts as you read them and save others to reread later? It's not only possible, but it's free, and it's easy.

Go to Feedly.com and create a free account. Click the plus sign in the left-hand pane and add the URL for a blog, podcast, or YouTube channel of choice. You can also enter a keyword to see what results appear. Click the *Follow* button as desired results appear.

Download the Feedly app to your phone. Start enjoying having the content you love delivered to one place.

My strategy is to scroll through the feed on my phone during spare moments in the day. I read the titles and decide what I really want to read. Swiping right saves a post to read later. The other posts, once the reader passes them by, will not show again.

When I am at my desktop computer, I go to Feedly and click *Read Later* in the left sidebar. All the links I selected on the phone to read later show in this section. All are marked with a green ribbon, indicating they have been saved to read later. As I finish with each one, I click the green ribbon to turn it clear. That article will now no longer appear.

Share with Remember The Milk

What about all the random articles we run across and want to review later? When viewing them on the phone, use the sharing icon. Once the Remember The Milk app is on the phone, Remember The Milk will show as one of the choices in the "share" menu.

Click the share icon. Choose Remember The Milk. Watch Remember The Milk open to a new task, insert the title of the article as the name of the task, and insert the URL for the article. All you have to do is save. You just earned the right to forget about the article. It's in Remember The Milk.

Text Expanders: Quicker and More Polite Replies

Have you received an email asking a question and spend 30 minutes crafting a gracious and masterful reply? The question was clearly explained in the student handbook, but you are the gracious school leader.

The second time an email brings the same question, the reply is likely not quite as masterful or gracious. By the time the ninth email brings the same question, it's all we can do to be halfway polite.

A text expander allows us to hit a couple of keys and watch that most eloquent four-paragraph reply appear. As this book goes to print, my choice is a free extension called "Text Blaze" (https://blaze.today) Search for that term in the Chrome Web Store and install it. The free version allows 20 shortcuts and works anywhere in the Chrome browser. It's perfect for Gmail, Google Drive, Microsoft 365 Online, Evernote Web, and social media platforms. It also includes shortcuts that insert the current date or time.

Here is a starter list for what to include in the text expander:

- **Your school name**. Think of how many times you key the entire name. Now, you'll accomplish the same with just a couple of keystrokes.

- **School address**. Include your name, school name, street address, city, state, and zip.

- **Your email address**. How many times have you included a typo when sending this address to someone else?

- **Date stamp**. Creates the current date. The extension allows you to define a variety of styles.

- **Date and time stamp**. Creates the current date and current time. This one would be good for taking notes when the exact time of the comment is important.

- **Answers to frequently asked questions.** Even though your patience may be gone, the shortcut provides that long, detail, eloquently-phrased answer every time.

- **List of faculty/staff names**. How many times do you need a check-off list? Now, you can insert one anywhere with a couple of keystrokes. (Be sure to add a yearly repeating task at the beginning of the school year to revisit and update the shortcut with names of new teachers.)

- **Ad hoc shortcut**. Often, a shortcut relates to an upcoming event. When the event is over, the shortcut is no longer needed. Change the wording to reflect the next "hot" topic.

 ## Gmail Templates

Gmail offers another way to handle frequently asked questions and common phrases. Gmail templates allow you to compose an entire email along with the subject line.

First, be sure *Templates* are enabled in the Gmail settings. Currently, that feature is found in the *Advanced* tab. To create a new template, open a new message and compose the subject line and the text.

Be sure to delete the signature line from that particular email. Otherwise, the template inserts an extra copy of the signature into the email message when using the template. After composing the template, click the three dots beside the trashcan and choose to save the draft.

To use a template, create a new message. Click the three dots. Choose the template from the list. Feel free to edit the message as needed. For example, you would want to personalize the greeting before sending.

 ## Gmail Filters

A text expander, such as Text Blaze, will insert multiple paragraphs of text. So why would someone also need Gmail templates?

Using a Gmail template allows the user to create a filter that will automatically send when certain emails arrive. Let's look at an example.

Remember Melanie and Savannah from Chapter 8? Savannah wants to hold a poetry contest at her school. Each participant will submit his/her poem in the body of an email message. Savannah would somehow like to save the poems together until the deadline and then read them all at once.

Also, she would like to send each participant an email with information on a special reception for everyone who enters. She wants each student to receive that email as soon as he/she submits an entry. How can Savannah automate the process?

First, let's give the students a special email address for submission. Suppose Savannah's Gmail address is savannah@gmail.com. She could give the students this address: savannah+poems@gmail.com. They will submit their poems to that address.

Next, Savannah will create and save a Gmail template. In it, she will compose the message students receive when they submit their poems. Then she will save that email as a Gmail template.

The next step is to create a filter that will take each newly arriving poem and batch them together. Savannah goes into the Gmail settings, finds the tab for *Filters and Blocked Addresses,* and then finds the link to *Create a new filter.*

How will Gmail know which emails contain a poem? They will be the messages sent to *savannah+poems@gmail.com.* So, Savannah puts that address in the "to" line of the filter. She now selects *Create filter* (Figure 9.5).

Gmail now wants to know what to do with emails that meet the criteria. Savannah wants three things to happen:

1   **She wants the emails to skip her inbox**. She doesn't want to handle each poem individually. She put a checkmark beside *Skip the Inbox (Archive it).*

2   **She wants the emails to be housed together**. She wants to read them all at one time. To achieve this aim, she checks *Apply the label.* From the dropdown, she adds a new label and names it *Poems.*

3   **She wants the student to receive an email**, the one she just composed and saved as a template. So, she also checks *Send template.* Savannah clicks the dropdown list and chooses her template. She clicks *Create filter* (Figure 9.6).

From	_____
To	_savannah+poems@gmail.com_____
Subject	_____
Has the words	_____
Doesn't have	_____
Size	greater than _____ ▼ _____ MB ___ ▼

☐ Has attachment   ☐ Don't include chat

Create filter | Search |

Figure 9.5 Example of a Gmail filter

◄ When a message is an exact match for your search criteria:

☐ Skip the inbox (Archive it)
☐ Mark as read
☐ Start it
☑ Apply the label: Choose label ▼
☐ Forward to: Choose an address ▼
☐ Delete it
☐ Never send it to Spam
☑ Send template: Choose template ▼
☐ Always mark it as important
☐ Never mark it as important
☐ Categorize as: Choose category ▼
    Also apply filter to 0 matching conversation

[Create filter]

Figure 9.6 Completing a Gmail filter

Savannah has freed herself from having to handle each poem individually. In fact, she has just automated the entire process. As emails arrive addressed to *savannah+poems@gmail.com*, Gmail archives them, applies the label, and sends each student an email. When Savannah is ready, she clicks the *Poems* label from the left sidebar, and sees the entire list of poems.

Voice Input: Why Type When You Can Talk?

One incredible timesaver is the ability to talk and let the technology automatically transcribe voice to text. On the keyboard for your mobile device, look for a key with a microphone icon. Tap it and talk. Writing an email with two thumbs on a piece of glass is a chore. Speaking the same email is a breeze. Use the same technique to compose social media posts and comment on the posts of others.

On your computer, voice input is also possible. Install the *Dictation for Gmail* Chrome extension. Notice the microphone icon at the bottom of the screen. Click it and speak your voice mail.

Composing a document in Google Docs? On the *Tools* menu, select *Voice typing*. Compose the document with your voice. What about Microsoft Word? On the *Home* tab, look for the *Dictate* button.

Otter.ai is another significant service. Create a free account and download the mobile app. As you speak, Otter translates voice to text. If you are part of a conversation, Otter also captures the input from the other parties. But then, it goes a step further. Otter recognizes voices and will identify which person is speaking at any point.

Otter is an outstanding tool for recording class lectures. It is perfect for conducting an interview and prevents misquoting. When recording a conversation with someone else, be sure to let the other party know.

Log into the Otter account on the desktop computer. Conversations and transcriptions created on the mobile app appear here as well. Copy and paste text into class notes, the interview article, or wherever the transcription needs to live permanently. The recordings and transcriptions can also remain in Otter. The mobile app allows export of conversation to email, Evernote, and many other services.

Proofread with Your Ears

Try as I may, I cannot proofread my own writing. My eyes see what my brain meant rather than what my finger actually did. If I read the text aloud, my success is better. But again, my tongue seems to say what my brain meant instead of what wound up on the page.

But if *someone else* reads the text aloud, my ears instantly perk up when something doesn't sound right. I have a free Chrome extension called *Read Aloud*. It's available in the Chrome Web Store.

Before I send an important email, publish a blog post, or leave a Google Drive document, I highlight several paragraphs, right-click and select *Read Aloud* from the menu. The extension allows the user to choose from several voices and adjust the pitch, volume, and speed.

When I am working in Microsoft Word, I use the built-in *Read Aloud* option located within the *Review* tab.

Write Like Hemingway

Readers and writers remember Ernest Hemingway for his short, powerful sentences. *Hemingway Editor* is a free website located at *hemingwayapp.com*. Paste the text and watch Hemingway Editor work its magic. It flags sentences it finds "hard to read" or "very hard to read." It flags passive voice and phrases where a simpler alternative is available. The site also highlights adverbs and gives a recommended limit for the amount of text. The site provides a word count and a reading level for the text.

Hemingway Editor and *Read Aloud* work hand in hand. Paste the text in Hemingway Editor. Start rewording to make the colored highlights disappear. I often find myself making two short sentences out of one long one. After satisfying Hemingway Editor, let *Read Aloud* read it back. Not only will your ears catch errors, but overuse of certain words will stand out. When you enjoy hearing your writing, others will likely enjoy reading it.

Hemingway Editor is an incredible tool for students. When I was in high school, my teacher was circling passive-voice sentences with a red pen and returning papers a week later. Hemingway Editor catches the same faults immediately. Students work to reword and make their own corrections on the spot. Why not let technology guide students?

They will find the more they use Hemingway Editor, the less they need it. They begin to sense what sentences the software will flag as "difficult to read." They will use fewer adverbs. They will develop a bias for active voice. The same will happen for you.

Hootsuite: Organizing Social Media

Regular communication is an important component of a successful social media program. Sending 20 back-to-back tweets in one sitting and then nothing for a week is no way to operate. With a free Hootsuite account, the school leader can compose messages in one batch but schedule each one to post at a certain time.

Sign up for a free account at Hootsuite.com. At present, a free account allows the user to connect up to three social accounts. Twitter, Instagram, and either Facebook or LinkedIn would be logical choices. The user can schedule a single message to all three accounts.

You also have another way to post one message to multiple platforms. Compose appropriate applets in *If This Then That*. For example, every Instagram post containing the school hashtag could also post to Twitter or to the school's Facebook page.

A second advantage of using Hootsuite is its use of "streams." Each stream appears as a column in Hootsuite. Streams are especially helpful in organizing Twitter. With so much activity on Twitter, relevant information often gets lost in the noise. To help me see what I want to see, I created four lists in Twitter: *Platinum, Gold, Silver,* and *Bronze.*

I assign to the *Platinum* list close friends and others whose tweets I never want to miss. The other three lists house people I follow in descending order of how valuable their content is to me.

In Hootsuite, I created four streams, one for each of the four lists. I make sure I read the *Platinum* stream. Depending on the available time, I may continue to the *Gold* list, *Silver* list, or *Bronze* list. Hootsuite allows me to use the time I have for Twitter to read the content most relevant to me. It saves time and increases productivity.

A second type of stream is the "Search Stream." Most any conference has a hashtag. Create a search stream in Hootsuite for that hashtag. You see a running list of every tweet referencing that event. Does your school have a hashtag? Create a search stream for that hashtag so you can always see what is being tweeted in the name of your school.

Why Don't They Teach That in School?

This area is one where people of all ages are still learning. It's an area that constantly changes and improves. Tools such as Hemingway Editor give students as young as elementary school an easy way to get feedback on their writing. An extension such as "Read Aloud" makes proofreading easy and fun. Otter.ai adds a new dimension to taking lecture notes. Other tools we discussed make input through speaking instead of typing a viable option.

Little by little, we can all recognize the repetitive, mundane tasks we perform. We can then start to ask the question, "Can technology automate this process for me?" More and more, the answer to that question is becoming, "Yes."

Next Steps

Be on the lookout for repetitive and mechanical processes. If the task seems like it is something that could be automated, it probably can be. Someone else has likely figured out how to do it, has written about it, and has posted somewhere only a Google search away.

This chapter has provided many tools. Start with one. Pick one tool and pick a day to devote some time to explore it and determine how you can use it.

Return to this chapter to add another tool and another as they meet your needs. Finally, realize new tools appear all the time. The one that helps you the most may not have even been created when this book went to press.

PART

IV

Conclusion and Challenge

School Is Not a Place

School is a gathering of learners. It's what we do, not where we are. And while those statements have always been true, they became painfully obvious in 2020, when the COVID-19 pandemic hit.

Had it not been for technology, many communities would not have had school at all. An old proverb states, "Necessity is the mother of invention." How true that statement became in 2020.

Daily procedures changed. It's hard to "pass your papers to the front of the row" when there are no rows and no papers. Even teachers who shunned technology became well versed with tools such as Google Classroom and Schoology. Parents who knew little about technology learned how to log into Zoom and Google Meet. Parents and children learned together. And often, it was the child teaching the parent.

Leadership for Remote Learning: Strategies for Success (Williamson & Blackburn, 2020) points out common problems families and schools faced during the pandemic:

- **Access to high-speed Internet**. In many urban and rural communities, 40 percent of families had no access to high-speed Internet connections.
- **Limited computer access at home**. Several school-aged children along with their parents were sharing a single computer. The situation made synchronous learning especially difficult.
- **Parental work schedules**. Providing adult supervision for online learning was difficult for many families.

DOI: 10.4324/9781003179719-15

- **Lack of teacher experience**. Most teachers had never taught an online course. Professional development in this area was in its infancy.

At Sherwood Academy in Albany, Georgia, students learned remotely during the spring of 2020. They returned to in-person learning that fall. Vicki Davis is a teacher at Sherwood and serves as director of instructional technology. Her advice is to "innovate like a turtle" (Education and Career News, 2020).

In addition to moving slowly and deliberately, Vicki Davis advocates for teachers having a small toolkit. The teachers must teach all students how to use the tools. Taking small steps, diminishing stress by making things easy, and injecting fun into online learning are keys. "If you lecture the whole time on Zoom, you've lost them," she says.

Through it all, schools and the families they served did the best they could with what they had. Little by little, their best got better.

Where Did It Begin?

We tend to think of "online education" or "distance learning" as being recent developments. According to the article "The history of online schooling" (OnlineSchools.org, 2021), this concept began in the mid-19th century during the development of the United States Postal Service. "Correspondence colleges" used the postal service to transport material back and forth from teacher to student.

We've come a long way since then. Feedback from teacher to student takes seconds rather than weeks. But one thing hasn't changed. Educators have done the best they could with what they had.

Where Are We Headed?

Will things go back to "normal"? Let's hope not. We have the potential for something better.

Average people who had never been on a video conference can hold their own in any Zoom meeting. Parents who could not be present at school due to physical restrictions or being stationed in another part of the country used to miss out. Now, they are a few mouse clicks away from conferencing with a teacher or watching their child perform on a stage.

School is a group of 20 students in the same room with a single teacher. School is also a group of students connected across the community or across the globe.

School is a group of principals gathering over pizza at the local pizzeria or on a Zoom session as they exchange ideas and support each other. School is the book in your hands or the words on the screen as you digest this material. School is a gathering of learners. Thanks to this digitally connected world, it comes in many forms.

Sabrina's Journey

Sabrina began the year wondering how she would stay on top of it all. Her grandfather had made it look so easy. But the world had changed. The circumstances she faced had changed. Along the way, she realized her procedures and her tools must also change:

- **She still receives over 100 emails a day**. What she learned made her the master of making decisions about emails. She now gets "in" back to "empty" every day.

- **Voice mail has diminished**. People find Sabrina handles email well. So, they rely more on email and less on rambling voice-mail messages. The voice mail Sabrina does receive winds up in her email transcribed into text. Returning calls in one afternoon batch keeps the pace moving and allows her more focus during the day.

- **Text messages find their way to her email**. Her communication is much more consolidated. People who need to reach her with legitimate emergencies have her mobile phone number. They can also contact her administrative assistant to find her.

- **Seemingly countless repeating tasks are never forgotten**. It's all trapped in her digital task list. Seeing all tasks in one place motivates her to delegate some and stop doing others.

- **Twitter is now the professional learning tool Sabrina originally envisioned**. Her digital task list links to any message she wants to review.

- **Waiting time is now never wasted time**. From her mobile phone, she can read the articles from her favorite blogs. All the posts go to one place.

- **Google Drive is now a place that makes sense**. The folder system is so logical she seldom has to rely on search. But when a search is needed, she is the master of combining search criteria.

- **Sabrina uses her camera differently**. Her grandfather used his pocket memo pad to take copious notes from blackboards during meetings. Sabrina snaps a picture of the whiteboard and reviews the results later in Evernote.

- **Highlights from books are consolidated**. The portions she highlighted from all the books she loves used to be scattered throughout the various bookcases in her life. Now, the digital highlights from all books are in one place.

- **Voice input into her digital task list has become a habit**. She notices many of the faculty members have also adopted this practice.

- **Sabrina's task list holds complete information**. When she looks at her digital task list to tackle the next item of the day, links to any supporting document, note or email are right in front of her.

- **Sabrina no longer tries to do everything at once**. She has developed a way to trap everything new, organize it later, and execute on it at the right time.

- **The parents in her school love Sabrina's weekly email**. They come to expect it every Friday. They have only one place to look to stay abreast of everything they need to know about what's happening at school.

As a young girl, Sabrina's grandfather had taught her a valuable lesson. When you are faced with circumstances, come up with procedures to handle those circumstances. That's the way he always did it.

Reflecting on her own career, she recalls countless times people use a different practice. Their circumstances change, yet their procedures stay the same. Nowhere has that revelation been truer than with technology.

Your Journey

The next time you hear someone say, "That's the way we've always done it," challenge them on it. What we find is that somewhere back in time, somebody was faced with circumstances. They put in place procedures to handle the circumstances they found. They did the best they could with what they had.

Our challenge is to do the best *we* can with what *we've* got...and today we have so much more.

As a young boy, my favorite show was "Batman." I was amazed not only that Batman had a computer, but that he could talk to the computer. Today, I do the same thing with the smart speaker in our living room.

Every Saturday morning, I watched George Jetson carry on phone conversations. But during his calls, he could see the other person on screen. Today, it's commonplace. Who knows where technology will take us another generation from now?

Past generations have ushered in each new year with a resolution to "get organized." Going forward, making the most of our time carries the resolve to "get organized...*digitally*."

References

Education and Career News (2020, November 21). "How Vicki Davis has personalized her students' remote learning experiences." Retrieved from www.educationandcareernews.com/education-technology/how-vicki-davis-has-personalized-her-students-remote-learning-experiences/

OnlineSchools.org (2021, April 8). "The history of online schooling." Retrieved from www.onlineschools.org/visual-academy/the-history-of-online-schooling/

Williamson R., & Blackburn, B. R. (2020). *Leadership for remote learning: Strategies for success*. Routledge.

Appendix
Digital Services
Referenced

- **Apple Notes**. https://icloud.com Take digital notes and organize them through iCloud.

- **Calendly**. https://calendly.com Allow other people to book appointments on an owner's calendar.

- **Constant Contact**. https://constantcontact.com Send mass emails, such as to all parents within the school. The user can see which emails bounce, which are opened, and which links are being clicked.

- **Doodle**. https://doodle.com Find a time when multiple people are all free to meet.

- **Dropbox**. https://dropbox.com Store digital documents, audio, video, photo, etc. in the cloud. Share with desired people. Access from any device when logged into Dropbox account.

- **Evernote**. https://evernote.com Take digital notes on any platform and access them from any device.

- **Evernote Web Clipper**. https://evernote.com/webclipper Use this Chrome extension to copy information from the Web and store within Evernote.

- **Excel**. https://office.com Spreadsheet software that is part of the Microsoft Office productivity suite.

- **Feedly**. https://feedly.com Bring together new content from many desired sites. Excellent for pulling together articles from favorite blogs, episodes from favorite podcasts, or videos from YouTube channels.

- **Gmail**. https://mail.google.com Email software which comes as part of a person's Google account.

- **Google Calendar**. https://calendar.google.com Digital calendar which comes as part of a person's Google account. Allows sharing of calendars and integration with many third-party tools.

- **Google Drive**. https://drive.google.com Cloud-based service primarily for composing and storing documents related to word processing, spreadsheet management, presentations, and forms.

- **Google Keep**. https://keep.google.com Take digital notes within Google account and access from any device.

- **Google Meet**. https://meet.google.com Conduct and participate in videoconferences with individuals or groups.

- **Google Voice**. https://voice.google.com A phone number supplied by Google that you can set to ring your mobile phone, landline, or both. Change the preferences at will. Give this number to others in place of your personal numbers.

- **Hemingway Editor**. https://hemingwayapp.com Check your writing for errors, grammar, and ease of readability.

- **Hootsuite**. https://hootsuite.com Compose, organize, and read content from various social media accounts. Schedule content to post later.

- **iCloud**. https://icloud.com Cloud-based service from Apple allowing storage of files accessible from any device.

- **If This Then That**. https://ifttt.com Compose "applets" allowing two or more services to work together. A condition on one service triggers a response on another.

- **Kindle Highlights**. https://read.amazon.com/notebook Bring highlighted notes from all Kindle books together.

- **Mailchimp**. https://mailchimp.com Send mass emails. Similar to Constant Contact.

- **Microsoft Word**. https://office.com Word processing software that is part of the Microsoft Office productivity suite.

- **One Note**. https://onenote.com Take digital notes and access them from any device. Similar to Evernote. It is from Microsoft and works well with other Microsoft Office products.

- **OneDrive**. https://onedrive.com Cloud-based storage from Microsoft allowing storage of files and is accessible from any device when logged into the OneDrive account.

- **Otter.ai**. https://otter.ai Record voice notes that are transcribed to text. The service recognizes different speakers and indicates in the transcription which person is speaking.

- **Outlook**. https://outlook.com Keep calendar, tasks, contacts, notes, and email in one piece of software. It is part of the Microsoft Office productivity suite.

- **PowerPoint.** https://office.com/launch/powerpoint Presentation software that is part of the Microsoft Office productivity suite.

- **Read Aloud**. https://chrome.google.com/webstore Highlight and listen to text being read to you with this Chrome extension.

- **Save to Google Drive**. https://chrome.google.com/webstore Use this Chrome extension to copy information from the Web and store within Google Drive.

- **Smore**. www.smore.com Send mass emails. Similar to Constant Contact or Mailchimp. It is especially geared to schools.

- **Text Blaze**. https://blaze.today Compose snippets and assign keyboard shortcuts. Entering a keyboard shortcut expands the text to the entire snippet.

- **Remember The Milk**. https://rememberthemilk.com Digital task manager for individuals or small teams.

- **Zoom**. https://zoom.us Conduct and participate in videoconferences with individuals or groups.

CPSIA information can be obtained
at www.ICGtesting.com
Printed in the USA
LVHW081253210122
709055LV00024B/159

9 781032 017075